More Memories

of

Derby

The publishers would like to thank the following companies for their

support in the production of this book

Main Sponsor
Mertrux Limited

Derby Markets

Derbyshire Fire and Rescue Service

Greenbank Terotech Limited

Mason Coatings plc

Methodist Homes

Moody & Woolley

Park Engineering (Derby) Limited

G. F. Tomlinson Group plc

First published in Great Britain by True North Books Ltd
England HX5 9AE

© **True North Books Limited 2000**

ISBN 1 903204 20 8

Text, design and origination by True North Books Limited
Printed and bound by The Amadeus Press Limited

More Memories

of

Derby

Editorial text by Andrew Mitchell

Edited by Tony Bowler

Contents

Introduction

The landscape of Derbyshire varies from the bleak moorlands of the north to the Trent lowlands in the south. With an area of 1,016 square miles it is divided into nine districts: Amber Valley, Bolsover, Chesterfield, Erewash, High Peak, North East Derbyshire, South Derbyshire, Derbyshire Dales and the city of Derby. It is with the city that this book, the latest in the 'Memories' series, centres its interest. Derby lies along the River Derwent at an important route focus at the southern end of the Pennines. It was a county borough from 1888 until 1974. The extent of the present district is 30 square miles. But these facts and figures are just background to a wealth of historical interest that is held in and around this jewel of the county.

Curry's Derby premises in the 1930s

During the Triassic period the foundations of the famous red clay, so vital to the pottery industry in later years, were being laid. Stone Age flints have been unearthed in neighbouring Chaddesden and Belper. There were stone circles uncovered at Arbor Low. Gold bracelets, bronze daggers and pottery have been found near the A564, dating back to nearly 2000 BC, but the site of our modern city was still woodland.

Derby was founded in the 9th century AD by the Danes as Deoraby, from which the present name is derived. 'Der' is a corruption of 'deer' and 'by' is the Norse for 'village'. Derby was the village where deer once roamed in large forests. However, the Romans were in the vicinity before then. Around 50 AD, they were scouring the peak District for lead deposits. Just northeast, at Little Chester, is the Roman site of Derventio. It protected five Roman roads. The most important of these was Ryknield Street that ran towards Chesterfield and Doncaster. The Romans stayed until the late 300s AD.

In prehistoric times, this was the lowest place where the Derwent could be forded, at the spot where Causey Bridge now stands. It provided a link between upland and lowland Britain. A marshy area, it was subject to flooding.

Green's shoe repair shop, London Road in the 1960s

During their stay they had built their timber barracks, bathhouses, central heating systems, shops, taverns and eating places. Roman wells were excavated at Little Chester, Marcus Street and in the gardens of St Paul's vicarage.

Today's Derby grew under the Normans. Henry de Ferrers ruled the area from his base at Tutbury Castle. His name lives on in local place names. Early Royal Charters were granted in 1154-56 and 1204. The manufacture of porcelain in the locality began in 1750. After a visit by George III in 1773, the town was granted a patent to mark the china with a crown, and the local product was to be forever known as Crown Derby. This became Royal Crown Derby with the blessing of Queen Victoria in 1890. Silk throwing, or spinning by machine, was introduced into the town from Italy in 1719. Many people in Derby were formerly employed in the manufacture of silk hosiery,

lace and cotton. Textile factories still have some importance in the city's economy.

A canal network helped Derby's early factories. In the 19th century the city became a major railway centre. Rail and aircraft engineering are also important industries in the city. Derby has large cattle markets. All Saints Church (the cathedral from 1927) has a tower, 210 feet high, built in 1509-27. A population of around 250,000 delights in the traditional links and the 21st century facilities that the city has to offer.

As a reader, opening the first page of 'More Memories of Derby', you are entering a time warp that will take you back over the decades of the last century. Whilst the links with earlier days are important to put everything into perspective, it is on more recent times that we will be concentrating. Brought to you by the magic of the camera, each photograph is enhanced by carefully

An early 1930s view of St Peter's Street looking towards the Market Head

researched captions. The text of these, both wry and informative, takes the reader beyond the image to mental pictures of a time that has gone forever. Yet, it is one that we can bring back by nudging the memory banks and recalling what it was that grandpa told us about when spinning the yarns of his youth. This book is not meant to be a dry historical tome, but one that unleashes waves of nostalgia. Join with the photographer and caption writer as you take a stroll along the memory lanes that take us from the elegance of the late Victorians promenading along London Road to the deregulated buses whizzing around the city centre. In between those days we can recall the times when Rudolf Valentino was the screen heartthrob and Lassie came home. Then there was the poverty of the depression years, because not all memories are fond ones. Add to that the losses in two world wars. But, there were many happier times. Recall the jolly days when we played tig in the park. Children ran gaily without the worries of

being regarded as the mini adults of the fashion world that they are today. Then, Anglesey was our foreign holiday destination.

The following pages will help you remember a time when you went to a soccer match and bantered with opposition supporters standing next to you. You are about to enter a world when the washing machine was a luxury and donkey stoning the front step was a work of art. This book will help you remember the taste of ginger beer and dandelion and burdock. Wind up record players scratched out melodies recorded on old 78s as we swooned to the sounds of Sinatra, Johnny Ray and Guy Mitchell. In those days we had pubs that sold ale you could taste and we played games of don, cribbage and dominoes' fives and threes. Turn off that newfangled digital TV and settle back in your favourite chair. It is time to think of Toni perms, trams and trolley buses on which you used to spend your shillings and pence. Let the nostalgic journey begin.

Street scenes

Soaring 212 feet into the air, All Saints has the second highest tower in the country. It was nearly a lot lower a few years before this photograph was taken. Standing proudly above the other buildings in the late 1940s, it had been clipped by a barrage balloon during the war that knocked the tip of one of its pinnacles. Fortunately, that was the full extent of the damage. The perpendicular tower is all that is left of the medieval church that dated back to the first millennium and was here until 1723. The tower itself is not that old. It was built in Tudor times. It bears an inscription 'young men and maidens' that some think mean that the tower was built at the request of bachelors and maidens of the parish. After the old church was demolished, the remodelling was overseen by Dr Hutchinson. He raised money from parishioners and such famous benefactors as Robert Walpole and Isaac Newton. The architect James Gibb created a classical beauty that has stood the test of time. Derby was a mainstay of the Protestant Church during the Reformation and was a supporter of the Parliamentarians in the Civil War. Derbyshire was a largely Catholic county, so the town was a religious oasis for a long time. It was not until the influx of Irish mill workers in the early 1800s that Catholicism made much impact on the town. In 1839, the Victorian Gothic styled St Mary's Church was built. All Saints grew in status in 1927 when it was reconsecrated as Derby Cathedral. To the left is Ye Olde Dolphin Inne. Dating from 1530, it is the city's oldest pub.

Right: The car on the left had made a long journey. It is sporting a Scottish number plate. The tram on Babington Lane had a shorter trip to make. It was a run that would only last for another two years before it was phased out. Seen in 1932, the Joseph Wright School of Art was at the corner of the junction with Gower Street. Wright was an artist for whom light and shade held a particular interest. He was one of the first to use the dark satanic mills of the Industrial Revolution as subjects. Some of his paintings that include the image of furnaces burning bright against the night sky are quite dramatic. He was born in 1734 at 23 Irongate. Wright learned the art of portrait painting under Thomas Hudson of London. His portrayal of the Derby Hunt attracted a series of private commissions from local worthies. They included Richard Arkwright, Jedediah Strutt, John Whitehurst and Erasmus Darwin. Joseph Wright died in Queen Street in 1797. Babington Lane was also home to Derby's first ever cinema. The Midland Electric Theatre, designed by Arthur Eastham, opened on 27 July 1910. Its 1,100 audience appreciated the splendour of the repro-duction fireplace and gallery, whilst enjoying the comfort of the cafe and lounge. The first talkie was shown in 1931, by which time it was called The Picture House. Renamed the Ritz in 1957, it showed its last film, 'Green Mares' Nest', on 27 August 1960. It was later demolished.

Bottom: The cyclist in front of the single decker Trent bus was just about to pass Jackson's hat and boot shop in 1936. The shop description fixes the scene into an era when some men wore strong boots in preference to shoes. They were safer and sturdier for work in the factories and engineering plants. Labourers needed them on the roads and in the fields. Others just wanted something that would wear well. Nearly every man wore something on his head when he went out to work or play, whether it was the basic flat cap or a natty, soft, wide-brimmed felt fedora. Even though the worst days of the depression had gone, not everyone was on easy street. On Tyneside, 200 from the ranks of the unemployed left Jarrow in the damp and chill of an October morning in a march that was to end in London over a month later. On the left hand side of Victoria Street stood Ranby's famous department store. Every town had its own particular favourite, but most of them failed to keep up with changing consumer demands. Although large in its own right, this sort of store did not have the financial clout to be able to mount a complete facelift. The premises are now just one of many Debenham stores across the country. What was a collection of 18th century buildings came under the big chain store's control in 1962.

Above: 'Ah Bisto' the bus seemed to be saying as it passed along The Spot at the end of St Peter's Street. No roast beef has ever been complete without the addition of the famous gravy. Adverts brought us the sight of the Bisto kids who sniffed at the delicious aroma in their picture on the tin. Two other little kids were having fun by the telephone boxes. Whilst mum was making a call they were about to see what they could find in the adjacent box. At one time these girls could have tried pressing button B on the big black box underneath the handset. Callers got connected by putting their pennies in the slot and pressing button A. However, if there was no reply, they got their money back by using the return button. Often they forgot. It was always worthwhile checking button B or the returned money tray when you entered a phone box. You never knew your luck! But isn't it nice to see little girls dressed like little girls? White ankle socks and neat skirts look much more appropriate than jeans or tracksuits and trainers. It is a pity that they did not grow up to dress their own offspring like children instead of fashion conscious mini adults. Since this photograph was taken the buildings on the right have gone to make way for the Eagle Centre. The Green Dragon, where you could get a pint of Burton Ale, bit the dust about the same time.

Above right: This is a marvellous view of the Borough Architect's handiwork. The Council House, Magistrates' Court and Police Station were all built to Charles Aslin's design. The view of Corporation Street was taken in the summer of 1949, not long after the official opening ceremony on 27 June, performed by Princess Elizabeth and Prince Philip. In less than three years, she would be the Queen. Aslin's creation had taken some time to come into being. Building work had started as far back as 1938 when the mayor, Alderman A Butler, laid the foundation stone. It was to be the final piece in the jigsaw of the town's redevelopment programme that had begun at the start of the decade. Completion date was supposed to be in 1941. However, our eyes turned towards Europe in September 1939 when the first war sirens sounded. Building programmes were put on hold as our attention was focused elsewhere. Work recommenced after a six month respite. But, it was not the council that moved in. The government requisitioned the building and, from 1942, it was occupied for four years by the RAF. There was still work to be done and progress was slow. Only when the town council heard that royalty was coming to cut the official tape was there any urgency to get it finished. The inscription on the front of the Council House shows the Roman numerals for 1941. That was wishful thinking!

This scene was captured looking from Derwent Street into Market Place. The imposing structure of the Guildhall dominates the busy square. The congested view shows us just how reliant we became on the motor car and bus as the 20th century developed. Market Place was a regular setting down and picking up spot from the days of horse drawn trams and hansom cabs. The type and volume of traffic might have changed, but the popularity of the square has not altered. It is still a regular meeting place for people coming into the city to link up with friends and relatives before setting off on a shopping expedition or a night out. It seemed to be the natural thing to do for all manner of groups and societies. Knots of cyclists got together here before bowling off along the county's country lanes for a day out. Keen walkers in their tweeds and stout shoes congregated in Market Place before their own bus or train journey to a foray into the Peak District and hills above Matlock and Bakewell. Many left their cars for the day in the square, much to the annoyance of people trying to park for an hour or so whilst they did their shopping. On carnival days gaily decorated floats used Market Place as the starting point for a procession that took them down to Markeaton Park. The face of the area changed greatly with the building of the New Assembly Rooms.

Bottom: Knots of people are in deep discussion on this day in 1933. Out in the great wide world there was interesting news to discuss. Great events were taking place. The German government building, the Reichstag, had been burned down. There was a diplomatic rift between England and Australia just because the Aussies were on the receiving end of some hostile fast bowling. The 'bodyline' tour proved that it was not only Poms who could whinge. Sir Malcolm Campbell was setting the world land speed record, Fred Perry won the US Open tennis championship, 'King Kong' was wowing cinema audiences and Mahatma Gandhi was on hunger strike. On a lighter note, women could enjoy the sheer luxury of Bear Brand stockings. At home, Derby was celebrating its new bus station. It was no ordinary piece of architecture. Art deco had come to the town. It originated in the 1920s and developed into a major style in western Europe and the United States during the 1930s. Its name was derived from the Exposition Internationale des Arts Décoratifs et Industriels Moderns, held in Paris in 1925. Thank goodness it was shortened! The distinguishing features of the style are simple, clean shapes, often with a streamlined look. The new bus station was part of the first phase of the town central improvement scheme. It was built by Gee, Walker & Slater to a design by CH Aslin and HV Lem Chester.

Right: In 1922 the photographer was standing on the top of the old Shot Tower. It was where lead shot was made. The tower was erected in 1809 and was 149 feet tall. The lead was melted at the top of the tower and then allowed to fall through perforations and become shot pellets. These were cooled by water at the bottom of the tower. Pulled down in 1932, it had

provided a good view of what we now call Osnabruck Square. Derby has been twinned with this German town since 1973. Osnabruck stands in the Rhineland. Close to a river, like Derby, it provided a link through our armed forces who were stationed there. It was also a good way to try to build bridges and put the memories of two wars behind us. Exchange visits for schoolchildren and dignitaries help both cities forge bonds and friendships that look to the future. It was too soon for such gestures in 1922. Then the square had the rounded shape of Uncle Tom's Cabin tea room in the centre. They are Trent buses that are passing by it. To the left, with its advert for John Players' cigarettes, we can see the Exchange Hotel. There you could get some real ale. Offilers Ales was a proper Derby drink. The Co-op building can just be seen at the top of the picture. The Albert Street bus depot is to the right of it.

and other media coverage that mean we know the royals intimately. Over a century ago there was a mystique about them. The official opening of the first two wards took place on 7 July 1894. The Duke and Duchess of Devonshire carried out the ceremony. Victoria's great-great granddaughter, Queen Elizabeth II, opened the Guy Pulvertaft Hand Centre in the infirmary in 1992. Derbyshire Royal Infirmary became a NHS Trust in 1994, a century after it opened.

Top: Derby is a city with a proud architectural history. Above HL Brown's watchmaker's shop, the Royal Hotel stands as a fine testament to the skills of the architect and the builder. Looking down Victoria Street, the Congregational church can be seen in the distance. Ranby's department store is to the right. This street stands near where Markeaton Brook flowed. For obvious

Above: This is one of the oldest photographs of Derbyshire Royal Infirmary still in existence. The long dresses of the Victorian women promenading along the A6, London Road, date from about 1898. It was an age of great houses and nannies taking babies for a walk. The foundation stone for the hospital was officially laid on 21 May 1891. It was no ordinary ceremony. Royalty was in attendance. Queen Victoria did not give the job to one of her many relatives. She came in person to use the ceremonial golden trowel. What a day that was. Her loyal subjects turned out in droves to see the greatest and most powerful woman in the world. She ruled a mighty empire and Britain ruled the waves. Since the death of her beloved husband, Albert, 30 years before, she had not often been seen in public. For most local residents, it was the only chance they would ever have to see their monarch in real life. Today we find that fascination with royalty rather quaint. We have become blasé about the monarchy because of television

reasons, the road was once called Brookside. Culverts had to be built to safeguard against underground flooding. In the early 1800s, the Corporation's Improvement Commission, under the chairmanship of William Strutt, did much to improve the state of the town, new bridges were built and, eventually, Victoria Street and the Royal Hotel appeared in the mid 1830s. This scene, from a century later, is a reminder of the last days of the trams. The tram tracks were no longer in use after 1934. However, the overhead cables buzzed with electricity for the trolley buses that ran along here until 1967. Across from the Royal, Burton's famous men's outfitters came to Derby in 1932. After the war, many a serviceman would be kitted out in his demob suit from here. The tailoring of Montague Burton would lead to a new phrase coming into everyday usage. Getting the full Monty meant putting on a complete set of new clothes. In the 1990s it was to come to mean the complete opposite!

Left: You could go down underground to spend a penny at The Spot. The public conveniences never appeared on any tourist's list of places to visit. When they were discovered they were welcome all the same! There have been many attempts to explain the origin of The Spot's place name. One theory is that a customer wanted to find the Derby Malthouse. He was shown the place on a map and it was pointed out when he was told, 'That's the spot.' It is just as likely an explanation as any other. The man hurrying across the street towards the toilets had better get a move on. If he dawdles any more the bus will have him and The Spot will mark his last goodbye. The long shadows falling across the street suggest it was a fine summer afternoon. All the shops had their canopies pulled down. They guarded goods in the window from fading or perishing. The awnings were also useful in more normal British weather. They kept the raindrops off our shoulders. As we stood on the pavement we could look across the street at the large number of British cars on our roads. Morris, Leyland, Rover and Austin models were just a few of those that kept us near the top of the world league of automobile production. The invasion from the Far East allied to the decline of the home car industry changed the scene from the late 1970s onward.

Above: The old chap on the right must have felt cold even on such a sunny day. In his flat cap and Crombie overcoat he was standing near the junction of St James Street and the Cornmarket. Across the road from him a policeman was on point duty. His white sleeves acted like a conductor bringing in the orchestra on cue. Instead of violins and a wind section to oversee he had lines of traffic to control. With one imperious sweep of his arm he could send cars off to the right or continue on down the road. A strongly raised arm, palm facing you, meant stop or else. What power he had. Unfortunately, there were only a couple of pushbikes on the move in this picture from the 1930s. He was reduced to being not much more than an early form of lollipop man. Perhaps it got busier for him later on that day. One of his colleagues was dismounting from his cycle further down the road. A bobby on a bike was a regular feature of policing. Community coppers knew everyone and the public had confidence in seeing them on their beats. Now they just give you a crime number down the phone line for your insurance company. These days the building in the distance belongs to the Derbyshire Building Society on Market Head. It used to be Barlow Taylor's. The Old Wine Vaults pub was next door, but that disappeared from the scene in 1971.

Above: This is the wide expanse that was Midland Road in the late 1930s. It led to the station, demolished in 1985, from near its junction with London Road. It was often a busy place with people scurrying to and from the trains. The George Hotel is on the left. If you were on the early side perhaps a short detour to the bar for a bottle of Offiler's Nut Brown Ale would pass the time nicely. The Clarendon Hotel was just beyond in case a traveller was tempted to make a double stop on the way to the station. Many of the names along this road were linked with the Midland Railway Company. As well as the street and station names, there were also the Midland Garage and Midland Hotel. Francis Thompson, the company's senior architect, designed the hotel. He was responsible for the impressive 1,050 feet station frontage. Typical of early Victorian designers, he built cast iron columns to hold the glass roof of the train shed. He also planned the engine sheds and workshops. This might just as well have been Thompson Road as Midland Road. The 1930s' scene shows that Derby was not too badly off in those late depression years. Goods were on display in the shops and people had the wherewithal to buy. Rolls Royce and Midland Railway had been busy, so there was not the same level of unemployment as faced by many other industrial towns that had felt the pinch.

Above right: Normanton Road photographed during the early 1940s. Even without the members of the 82nd Airborne Division walking along the pavement, there are other clues to tell us that this is during the time of World War II. There is not a single car on the road. Petrol rationing meant that only essential journeys could be undertaken. The days of nipping into town or bowling out into the countryside in your Ford 8 were things of the past. Fortunately, they would also be of the future. However, the dreaded ration coupon meant that the whole of the decade was a poor time for the motorist. The other major pointers to the date can be found on the lampposts, telegraph poles and trolley car cable posts. They have white bands painted on them. In some places, especially at street corners, there would be paint on the kerbside. These marks were to help vehicles move around town during the blackout. No streetlights or illuminated shop fronts were allowed in those days or the Luftwaffe would have a marked target for its bombs. 'Put that light out!' was the cry from the Air Raid Wardens if so much as a chink of light came through our curtains. The Technical College is on the left of the bend and Christ Church is just further along. It was built in 1838 and has the highest steeple in the town.

In the 18th and 19th centuries there were many coaching inns dotted around Derby. They provided refreshment and comfortable stopovers for weary travellers. They were also places where a change of horses could be obtained. The George (Irongate), Tiger Inn (Corn Market), Nag's Head (St Peter's Street) and New Inn (King Street) were some of the more famous ones. Another with a long coaching history is the Bell Inn on Sadlergate, dating from 1680. Its large yard is an obvious reminder of the days when the horse drawn stagecoaches swung in through its gates with a dusty and tired set of passengers making the long journey to the capital. The Derby Canal Company held its inaugural meeting here in July 1793. This scene was captured in 1965. For a long time the Bell had a men only bar. It was popular with old timers who gave short shrift to any feminist or emancipated woman who dared to cross the threshold. This bar, the Tudor Bar, was the last bastion of male dominance. In its smoky atmosphere the men could drink, curse and play three card brag, bones, solo, nap and fives and threes to their hearts' content, all to the backdrop of a fine collection of arms and armour. They could also exchange the sort of banter that would have made their wives blush. There was one exception to the no female rule. When the Salvation Army came round selling the 'War Cry' a female member of the 'Sally Army' was allowed in. Not only that, she was afforded respect. Any man who attempted to embarrass her was put firmly in his place. There were limits.

High days & holidays

The old chap on the right is taking a moment to collect his thoughts on the park bench in the River Gardens. The centrepiece he is gazing at is no longer there. It has been moved to Allestree Hall. In the 1940s he could sit there and think of the world that he had fought to create in the 1914-18 war. Many of his mates had been left behind in the mud of Flanders and the Somme. Now it was the turn of his sons to try to make it a better place for the little tot and her mum gazing at the fish and the lily pads in the pool. The goldfish swimming in and out of the stone turtles made it a pretty spot for youngsters to enjoy. The Derwent embankment and gardens were opened to the public on 10 November 1933. It was a beautiful place to come to at lunchtime and leave the cares of the office behind for just an hour. Clerks and secretaries from the typing pool brought their sandwiches and sat on the steps watching the swans and ducks glide by. Every so often there was a frenzy of action as the birds raced to collect a crust thrown their way, before they resumed their graceful passage down river. After lunch, the office workers often took a stroll in the nearby open market before heading back to their desks and shorthand pads.

The Alexandra is a common name on cinemas, theatres and hotels throughout the country. They all owe their name to Queen Alexandra, the wife of King Edward VII. The eldest daughter of Christian IX of Denmark was a woman of exceptional beauty and grace. She became an immediate and lasting favourite with the British public. The Alexandra on Normanton Road began life as a ice skating rink. It was converted to a cinema in 1913. Silent movies, with captions to describe the action, became very popular in a short time. Piano playing from the pit of the auditorium enhanced the mood. Crashing crescendos greeted the climax of a scene and delicate tinkling accompanied a more romantic moment. It was renamed the Alex in 1939. By then, Derby filmgoers had adopted the national habit of entering the cinema at any old time. They would arrive halfway through a film. As it was shown twice in an evening, they sat there until it started again. Then they watched the beginning having already seen the end. By the time the plot reached the middle everything was revealed. Either that or they came out in utter confusion. It is little wonder that their children became Teddy boys and the crazy mixed up kids of the 1950s! The last film was shown in 1953 and it briefly became a roller skating rink again before changing to be the Trocadero Ballroom. Bingo came to call in the 1960s, but two fires in 1982 saw it close its doors forever.

Above: Derby's children have been enjoying the facilities at Markeaton Park for 70 years. Here they were cooling off in the age old way of frolicking, doggy paddling and splashing about. The girls were forced to wear bathing caps by mums worried that they might get split ends or catch a cold. They were also fearful that their daughters might catch some form of headlice and have to face Nitty Nora, the school nurse, on Monday morning. How the dreaded little creatures, the lice not the children, managed to swim from one head to another or why boys did not require similar protection has never been properly explained. It is just part of the wonderful eccentricity that is England. In the late 1960s and early 1970s lads' hair was halfway down their backs and the girls had theirs bobbed short. Other than in professional swimming races, bathing caps disappeared into the folklore of British costume. Markeaton Park was created from land bequeathed to the borough by Emily Mundy in 1929. The corporation bought up 180 acres of surrounding land and opened it to the public in 1931. Prince Albert, Duke of York, performed the opening ceremony. The Mundy mansion was used as a café, but it proved to be unsafe and the café was moved to a former Royal Artillery building before moving again to the orangery. Markeaton Hall was demolished in 1964. The lake opened in 1934 and there are now other entertainments in the park to amuse young and old. Crazy golf, boating, a light railway and kiddies' car circuit are just some of the diversions that the park has to offer.

Above right: If you are young, let your imagination run free. If you are not in the first flush of youth cast your mind back to days of Swallows and Amazons, Biggles' books and the Famous Five. Coming out of the Venezuelan jungle, beating a path through the muddy waters of the mighty Churun, the intrepid band of explorers gazes anxiously ahead at the bend in the river. Ahead of them they can hear the thunderous roar of the awesome Angel Falls. With their hearts in their mouths, our heroes pull for the river bank for all they are worth. If you have never played that game by letting your fancy run free, then you had a sad childhood. One of the pleasures of the lake at Markeaton Park was the ability to forget where you were and let your mind take you on an adventure that was yours for just a tanner a ride. Let those without any soul tell you the statistics. The anoraks of this world are free to know that the lake opened in 1934 by Alderman Herbert Stanley and was extended to seven acres in 1936. They can record that the SS Mundy was put in the play centre in 1971 as a storage area for boats and canoes. When they tell you that the lake is supplied with water from Markeaton Brook and is a great place for sticklebacks and minnows, tell them it is nonsense. This is a tributary of the River Caroni and those are piranha and crocodiles.

Didn't we have a lovely time...

In the days before television brought entertainment into our homes, there were cinemas and theatres for us to visit. We had radios, but the imagination can only do so much. We needed to see our entertainment, not just hear it. Even if it was on film it still felt as if we were close to the top stars who could thrill us, amuse us or make us dab a the corner of our eye with a discreet handkerchief. Before the days of the movie screen, our ancestors enjoyed watching jugglers and tumblers perform their acrobatics in public spaces. They could also watch dreadful cockfights and other bloodthirsty pastimes, but we had better gloss over those. There is a record of a tightrope walker who, in 1732, performed on a wire between the towers of All Saints and St Michael's. He came down at such a rate that smoke was seen billowing in his path. It came as no shock to learn that he was killed in Shrewsbury a few weeks later, trying to perform a similar stunt. The Assembly Rooms became an entertainment centre for the upper crust in the 18th century. There was a handsome ballroom and a card room for those who liked a hand of whist. The first permanent theatre in the town was established on Bold Lane, although travelling bands of players had performed in the courtyard of County Hall in earlier times. In the Victorian era, attempts were made to uplift the masses by providing interesting lectures at the Mechanics Institute. Mrs Clara Balfour was surprised that hordes did not flock to listen to her discuss the 'Intellectual Influence of Women in Society'! The general public preferred to go to Princes Street to see Keith's Circus. The same street also boasted the Star Music Hall, another popular place of entertainment. The lively and rather rough Palace of Varieties was also a music hall. It opened in 1897.

For those who wanted entertainment at a level in between the music hall and the boredom of Mrs Balfour, the Grand Theatre in Babington Lane was the answer. It opened in 1885 and was popular for its pantomimes and plays. One very successful production was 'The Sign of the Cross'. Trainloads came to see it from far and wide. It was supposed to be a story of the early Christians, but it was a scene that included semi naked wenches in an orgy scene that attracted the crowds! By the early 20th century the Hippodrome

Variety Theatre, the Empire and Coliseum Music Hall had opened. Comedians, singers and speciality acts thrilled the audiences in twice nightly shows. Although live entertainment continued to flourish until the second world war, there was increasing competition from the new attraction of the age of electricity. The moving picture had arrived.

In the years when Theda Bara was vamping her way across the screen and Douglas Fairbanks was swashbuckling for all his worth, the cinema became a firmly established favourite. By the time that the first talkie was shown at the Cosmo in Boundary Road, there were 14 cinemas in and around the town. The Cosmo had opened in the 1900s as a public hall named the Cosmopolitan. It sounded much more modern to the audiences of 1923 when its name was shortened and silent movies were first shown there. It lived up to its full name in later life when it began showing Asian films in its later years, though it was renamed the Meena. It closed in 1979. Other famous names from the Cosmo's early days include East Street's Regal, the Popular in Mill Street and the Gloria in Chaddesden. Many places showed the early magic lantern slide shows and the first movie reels. Large halls at the Mechanics Institute, Albert Hall, Central Hall, Drill Hall, the Palace Variety Theatre and Normanton Pavilion were all given over to showing the latest entertainment fad.

But, the very first purpose built cinema was the Midland Electric Theatre, Babington Lane. The projector flickered into life on 27 July 1910. It became the Picture House in 1913. The original name only lasted three years. Strangely, its last name would die after the same length of time. In 1957 it became the Ritz and closed in 1960. It had been built on the site of the old Babington Hall and boasted a marvellous fireplace and staircase.

Cinema audiences fell dramatically when television entered the entertainment arena. Many cinemas became bingo halls or clubs. Some just disappeared. By 1977 there were just three left. Young people found other back rows in which to do their courting.

In Staffordshire the Romans built roads through the forests that covered the county, including what are now Watling Street and Ryknield Street, intersecting near Lichfield. Derby had its own Ryknield Street. It ran to Chesterfield and Doncaster, from Little Chester, the district just north of the city centre. A Roman well, found just off the path of the old Roman road, shows that it was a spot where travellers could water their horses and refresh themselves before continuing on their way. The name lives on in the slightly altered spelling of Rykneld Road, part of the A5250 that carries traffic from the city to the A38 and southwest to Burton upon Trent. Rykneld Recreation Ground maintained the historic

links. It was given a play area and large paddling pool, well resourced playground and open spaces for soccer and cricket. Residents of the densely populated housing nearby were happy to use the facilities every chance they got. Children lost any fear of water by splashing and skylarking in the pool. The girl standing up, fixing her hair, was a little older than her playmates. She was developing the female version of posing when this picture was taken. Did she go on to be a fully fledged poser? Only she will know. If she doesn't, her pals will tell her. In the early 1950s such paddling pools were greeted with suspicion. The polio epidemic made parents worry about their children catching this contagious disease.

Left: Zanzibar is a nightclub that is regarded as one of the best in the Midlands. It stands on the site of the Gaumont Palace cinema, seen here on the west side of London Road. It was photographed after the tramlines had been covered over and dates from about 1935. Going to the pictures was a Friday night treat for courting couples. On Saturday they went dancing, but Friday was devoted to the silver screen. Cuddled up on the back row with your sweetheart, you could imagine it was Errol Flynn holding your hand, almost. If the lights were down then he had a chance. He might have been a bit of a disappointment when the lights went up, but he had bought the tickets and paid for the ice cream. He had some good points. Never trust a lad who said, 'I'll meet you inside.' Marry that sort and you would never see the inside of his wage packet. You got value for money at the cinema when we were young. There was the main feature and a 'B' film as well. Sometimes you got a cartoon and a cheery message at the end with 'That's all folks'. We kept up to date with the news and stood for the National Anthem before heading for home. The star of 'Little Friend' was Matheson Lang. He was a Shakespearean actor better known on the stage than in films. He had started the Shakespeare seasons at London's Old Vic. He died in 1948. His co-star, Nova Pilbeam, appeared in other films, such as 'Young and Innocent'.

Below: This is the magnificent interior of the Gaumont Palace. The cinema opened in 1934. The art deco design was popular between the wars. Decorative ideas came from American Indian, Egyptian and early classical sources as well as from nature. Characteristic motifs included nude female figures, animals, foliage, and sunrays, all in conventionalised forms. The Gaumont Palace featured a number of these, but drew the line at the naked form! In 1965 the cinema became known as the Odeon and then the Trocadero. When it ran its final reel on 17 December 1988 it was called Cannon. One of its most distinctive features was the marvellous Compton organ. Music from its pipes entertained audiences before the start of the evening's films and, again, during the interval when the usherettes were bringing round the ice cream. The organ was sold to St Philip's Church, Chaddesden in 1965. There it played 'For those in peril on the sea' rather than 'Shrimp boats are a-coming'. When the Gaumont Palace opened we were a nation of cinema goers who thrilled at the celluloid stars of Hollywood. The glamorous Swede, Greta Garbo, entranced us in the mid 1930s with 'Queen Christina' and 'Anna Karenina'. Who could ever forget the impact of our own Ronald Colman in 'A Tale of Two Cities'? When he said, 'It is a far, far better thing I do now,' there was not a dry eye in the house as he took the long walk to the guillotine.

Above: The Wembley trail stopped winding for Derby County on 27 April 1946. Until then, and ever since, the twists and turns of that famous journey to lift the FA Cup have frustrated our heroes. The trail lasts a little longer these days, as the final now comes in the second half of May. There are also various European finals to be played. In 1946 the FA Cup Final was the last match and high spot of the season. That first competition after the war tried to satisfy the massive interest in the return of professional sport. The early rounds were played over two legs, with the aggregate goals total determining the winner. Everything started nicely as Luton Town was swept aside in the third round. The top clubs were exempt from the first two rounds. Next came victories over West Bromwich Albion and Brighton. The sixth round tie against Aston

Villa was a ding dong struggle. The Rams scraped through by the odd goal. The semi final against Birmingham was won after a replay in front of a record crowd. Then it was on to the big day. Burglars would have had a field day in the town as it emptied for the pilgrimage to the Mecca of soccer. The final went to extra time before Derby could claim its 4-1 victory over plucky Charlton and Jack Nicholas could hold the Cup aloft. An official reception was held the following Tuesday and the team paraded the Cup through the streets on its way to the function.

Back row: J Bullions, J Nicholas, V Woodley, L Leuty, J Howe, W Musson.

Front row: S McMillan (manager), R Harrison, H Carter, J Stamps, P Doherty, D Duncan, D Willis (trainer).

From baseball to a sense of pride

Baseball, rams, bloomer, clough, pride and a bald eagle is an odd selection of words. Stranger still is the connection they have with football. But, to a Derby County supporter, they speak volumes. They are part of proud traditions of the soccer club that was one of the 12 founder members of the Football League. Baseball is a sport that makes us think of the Chicago White Sox or the Milwaukee Brewers, teams from across the great pond. But, baseball teams played in Derby in the 19th century. Industrialist Francis Ley had been a fan of the sport and this Baseball Ground became our soccer club's home from 1895 right through to 1997. Rams to outsiders are merely sheep with big horns, but they are the symbol and nickname of our beloved club. Bloomer is nothing to do with the woman who invented the large knickerbockers for cyclists, but the name of Derby's first superstar. Steve Bloomer was the top scorer for 13 consecutive seasons, from 1893-94 to 1905-06. An exciting striker, his goal tally of over 300 may never be beaten. He also scored 28 times for England in just 23 games. Clough and bald eagle are nothing to do with a ravine or the national bird of America. Brian Clough is the manager who guided Derby County to its first Division One league title and 'bald eagle' is the affectionate nickname given to Jim Smith who came to manage the Rams in 1995 and saw them into the 21st century back in the top flight of English soccer. Derby County had its pride restored when that happened, playing, as it now does, at its new home of Pride Park in a modern 33,000-seater stadium.

Football is now big business. When Derby County began its life as an offshoot of the county cricket club, who would have believed that football players would become millionaires and that selling replica shirts and hospitality packages would become more important than the match receipts? When Steve Bloomer was rampaging through defences, and Jack Bowers was following him into the record books in the 1930s, it was a game with which the working man could identify.

Standing on the terraces on a windswept and rainy November afternoon, he saw men who earned a similar wage and came from the same sort of background. Clutching a cup of Bovril, he knew that he might bump into the team's right fullback on the top deck of the bus home.

During the 1930s, the Rams were runners up in Division One on three occasions. Their luck in winning a top trophy changed after the war. In the FA Cup Final of 1946, County sent a strong team to Wembley to play Charlton Athletic. Included in the team were two legends of that or any era. Peter Doherty and Raich Carter were amongst the finest inside forwards that ever played in this country. Today's players would find it hard to match this pair's silky skills with a muddy, leather football. Charlton was swept aside 4-1, but quiz buffs will remember the final because the ball burst during the match. Amazingly, the same thing had happened in a League game the previous Wednesday against the same opponents! Two of the goals scored that day came from Jackie Stamps, a brave centre forward whose best years were lost to the war. A bar and eating place in the city centre keeps his name alive.

Derby County had its proudest moments in the early 1970s. The controversial Brian Clough built a team that was to win the Division One title in 1971-72. The team went on to reach the European Cup semi final the following season. Clough's successor, Dave Mackay, took Derby back to the top in 1974-75, but the team had seen its best days. Tommy Docherty, the man with 'more clubs than Jack Nicklaus', had managed Manchester United to relegation a few years earlier. He succeeded Mackay and helped the Rams follow United's path. Docherty even sold Kevin Hector, the club's best goalscorer for 70 years!

After being in the doldrums, it was good to see the old club back in the big time. Now all we need is another Bloomer or Hector to score the goals to keep us there.

season to the same as that of a lesser light. When he stated that he was a better player, the manager retorted, 'Not in the summer, you're not!' Jimmy Bullions played in an era when medals meant more than money. It was just as well.

Above: Jack Howe was the left fullback in Derby County's FA Cup winning team of 1946. The magnificent trophy looks a little odd placed on the old dining room chair, but Jack and his young admirer would not have cared. This was a day to be proud of, one to be remembered for the rest of their lives. Jack Howe had a cup winner's medal that so many other more famous names would miss out on. That magical player of the 1960s, George Best, never even played in a Wembley final, much less won a medal. So, Jack had something that others would have given their eyeteeth for. He belonged to a time when shorts were baggy and haircuts came from the short back and sides school of barbering. Jack was also a defender who was just that. Not for him the tactical formations of wing backs and sweepers. His job was to mark the other side's winger with a 'he shall not pass' attitude. One good crunching tackle in the first five minutes made the next 85 that much easier. Sometimes, it was easier said than done. There were players around like Stanley Matthews and Tom Finney. It was all right giving them a tough time, the problem was catching them! When Jack won his medal it was a time when football grounds were nearly overflowing. The war years had starved the public of sporting entertainment. Crowds flocked in to see their favourites in that first postwar season.

Above: Jimmy Bullions was one of only two members of Derby County's 1946 FA Cup winning team to survive into the 21st century. A powerful right half, he was very much a man's man. Strong on stamina and not short on skill, he was in the engine room that gave the likes of Peter Doherty the room to weave more delicate patterns further upfield. In Jimmy's day, players stuck very much to a rigid formation of play. They had a specific job to do and woe betide a player who tried anything too fancy. It was not easy to be too clever. The heavy boots they wore and the leather football they kicked soon became heavier still if the conditions were muddy. In the typical winter of a British season there were many matches where it was survival of the fittest. Heading that sodden ball was an act of bravery as well as skill. Many a player had stars in his eyes after meeting a leather cannonball with his forehead. And

what was Jimmy's reward for stardom? His wages were just a few pounds a week. Once, an international player went to ask the manager why his wage had been cut in the close

Left: The Baseball Ground played host to the Rams until the day that this photograph was taken. A new home at Pride Park was ready. Its brand spanking new facilities were ready. Died in the wool County fans could only hope that the bad old days of the 1980s, when the club even slipped into the old Division Three for a while, would not return. The final match was played on Sunday 11 May 1997. Mascots David and Sam Bowler had made the long journey from Poole for the honour of being on the field. Substitute Dean Yates posed with them.

Hip, hip, hooray for the Duke of York. The 38 year old second son of George V was paying a visit to Ley's foundries. The happy, mainly female, band of workers had been graced by the royal visit. In 1933 there was a love of the family that kept us truly British. Not for us the presidents and republics that many other European nations had. We had a monarchy and even an empire. The women were proud of their heritage and whooped and cheered loudly to let the Duke know what they felt. Their company founder, Sir Francis Ley, set up his Vulcan Foundry in 1874, close to the railway line, so making access for raw materials and finished goods that much easier. The Derby and Birmingham branch of the Midland Railway Company, the LNWR, Great Northern and North Staffordshire Railway Companies were all linked to the works. This helped the business prosper. 'Where there is muck, there's brass,' they used to say. Never was it truer than at Ley's. Steam billowing from the locomotives mixed with smoke from the foundries as sweat and grime turned into hard cash. Famous for its 'Blackheart' castings, Ley's company expanded rapidly and was greatly extended in 1897. The firm's giant water tower was a famous landmark. There was a special subway system in the works' yard. It held the drains and carried gas, water and electric cabling. Eventually, as industrial times changed, the company was taken over by William's Holdings in 1982. It was then sold on to Haleworth Holdings, but closed its doors in April 1987.

Memorable moments

Above: Jolly bunting was waving in the breeze on 12 October 1936 as the crowd waved goodbye to the royal visitor. Men lifted their hats out of respect and women applauded the little procession of cars that were leaving the grounds of Derbyshire Royal Infirmary. Nurses bobbed a little curtsey and then returned to the wards. The bunting was quite useful in 1936. It came out to mark the accession of the new king, Edward VIII. Having been carefully put away, it might well have been brought out again towards the end of the year to welcome George VI as his brother abdicated in December. The uncrowned king was keeping a low profile when the foundation stone was laid for new extensions to the infirmary. The general public was largely ignorant of his affair with the twice married American socialite, Wallis Simpson. At Westminster, the corridors of power were awash with the pros and cons of such a woman becoming Queen. It was Edward's sister in law, Alice, who performed the ceremony. She was married to Henry, Duke of Gloucester. The Duchess was well received when she set in motion the building of G Block. It was to house a number of new wards. When it was completed in 1938, at a cost of £90,000, Edward VIII had become the Duke of Windsor and married the woman who nearly brought down the monarchy. They continued to be controversial, especially when they had a friendly meeting with Adolf Hitler. During the war they were packed off to the Bahamas.

A crowd of excited workers and onlookers waves goodbye to the Duke of York after his visit to Ley's Malleable Casting Co Ltd. It was 3 May 1933 and a time when a royal visit meant so much to the British public. There was no television in those days and the only sight people had of the royals was from Pathé newsreels at the cinema. To have a chance to see a member of the Windsor family in the flesh was not one to be missed. Babies were dragged along in their prams and necks were craned for a better look. Britain was still feeling the effects of the depression, so it was good to have something to cheer about. Across the Channel some new chap called Hitler had just

become Germany's Chancellor. He was a funny looking little bloke. We did not think that he would have the same sort of significance as our beloved royals. Little did we know that the Duke of York would have a major part to play in our history. In 1933 he was just the brother of the future king. He had two pretty daughters, Elizabeth and Margaret, who would live out a life as minor princesses. All that would change three years later. The Duke of York would be thrust on to the throne when his brother, Edward VIII abdicated. The visitor to Ley's would be our George VI and his daughter was to be Queen Elizabeth II. Who in the crowd could have seen what lay ahead?

Bottom: The uniforms of the nurses look almost Victorian in style. It would be easy to think that Florence Nightingale was about to appear clutching her magic lamp. The long aprons and starched caps belong to a much later time. It was 1936 and the two women walking down the aisle between the ranks of nursing staff were on an informal tour of inspection. The nurses were forming a guard of honour for the Duchess of Gloucester on her visit to Derbyshire Royal Infirmary. By her side was Ellen Kenyon. She was the hospital's highly respected, and not to be trifled with, matron. Lady Inglefield, the infirmary's president, was also in the party, but she had been delayed talking to some of the other staff further down the line. It was a proud day for these angels of mercy who were standing politely as the official entourage went by. Their dedication had been recognised in the Duchess's official speech at the ceremony that marked the opening of this extension to the infirmary. The women worked long hours dealing with many distressing cases. Nursing never has been a job or an occupation. It is a true vocation where people put the needs of others before their own. Their hearts warmed to the King's sister in law when she said that the whole country was grateful for the work that they did. It is nice to be appreciated.

Left: On 12 October 1936 the Duchess of Gloucester might have been forgiven if her thoughts were elsewhere. The behaviour of her brother in law, David, was causing the family some concern. Another brother in law, Bertie, always a nervy individual, was on tenterhooks. Friends and relations knew David by the last of his seven Christian names. To the general public he was King Edward VIII and he was about to abdicate. Ironically, brother Bertie used his last name only when he succeeded to the throne as George VI. The Duchess was one of a breed of the stiff upper lip classes that made sure that the show went on, come what may. Lady Alice Montagu Douglas Scott had her own fair share of names when she married Henry, George V's fourth child. She carried our royal duties on behalf of the monarchy and is seen here laying the foundation stone for the new extensions to Derby Royal Infirmary. The scene was a mixture of pomp and practicality. Flowers and ferns decorated the dais whilst steel girders loomed in the background. The old microphone and stand through which the Duchess addressed the gathered crowd looks a real period piece to those of us used to modern radio mikes and tiny clip on pieces that presenters wear on their ties or blouses. Corporation dignitaries made sure that they got their faces seen and their wives produced their best fur coats for the occasion. As well as being a service of dedication for the hospital, it was also an opportunity to let lesser mortals appreciate their importance.

Above: The 1949 New Zealand touring cricket team had come to Queen Park, Chesterfield, before its match with Derbyshire. A charming floral display had been prepared on the lawn to welcome skipper Walter Hadlee and his teammates. Walter went on to become a senior administrator in Kiwi cricket. His sons inherited his love of the game. The most famous of them, Richard, became one of the all time greats. His smooth, flowing action was the role model for other fast bowlers of the 1970s and 1980s as he amassed a world record number of Test wickets that has only been bettered by a couple of others since. In 1949 the touring party had taken the long boat journey from New Zealand. International travel by plane was still in its infancy. The Kiwis followed Bradman's powerful Aussie side that had been over the year before. However, they were the minnows of Test cricket. The side did not manage to win a Test match until 1955-56 when a victory in Auckland over West Indies broke its duck. In the previous season, on the same ground, England had skittled out New Zealand for 26, a record low that still stands. It had a mighty hitter in John Reid, who once hit 15 sixes in one match. But, it was the rise of bowlers like Hadlee and such top class batsmen as Glenn Turner and Martin Crowe that helped the little nation become more of a force in world cricket in the last quarter of the century.

Below centre: On 27 June 1949 this fresh faced 23 year old attracted large crowds to welcome her to the town. Elegantly dressed, she had come to perform the opening ceremony at the Council House. Having been requisitioned by the military for the duration of the war, it had only recently been handed back to the town. The mayor, Alderman Charles Frederick Bowmer, and his lady wife graciously greeted Princess Elizabeth as the heir to the throne. Elizabeth's future loyal subjects craned their necks to get a better look. Children carried little flags that they waved as she passed by. Some of those had been brandished in the street parties on VE day, just four years previously. Thrifty people did not throw away anything that might have a future use! The royal princess had only been married to 28 year old Philip Mountbatten, Prince of Greece and Denmark, for 18 months. He gave up his right to those thrones and took his mother's surname when they got engaged. Philip became the Duke of Edinburgh when they married in November 1947. Princess Elizabeth was already a mother. Her first child, Charles, was seven months old when she came to Derby. On this happy day she could not have imagined the changes that would affect her family life in the second half of the century. Three of her children's marriages would end in divorce, as did that of her sister Margaret, and criticising the monarchy became a popular press pastime.

Market Place was the focal point for many civic events. Ceremonies of dedication have been held at the War Memorial and important announcements made outside the Guildhall. Another fine memorial, designed by Lutyens, stands on Midland Road. The assembled ranks of servicemen and women act as a reminder to us all of the debt we owe to these brave souls. There have been many conflicts that have taken our sons and daughters to foreign shores. Each decade seems to throw up another. In the 1990s it was the Gulf War and the 1980s sent us to the Falklands. Our troops were in Ireland in the 60s and 70s and Korea the decade before. We began the century with soldiers in South Africa. However, it is

the two world wars that had the greatest impact on our lives and development, even if they are several generations removed for the youngest of us. In the 1914-18 war many joined up with the Sherwood Foresters Regiment. The shocking statistic that 11,409 men from this regiment alone were killed in action is enough to make you stop in disbelief. The war cost 1,000,000 lives from British Empire combatants. To think we did it all again just over 20 years later seems incredible. This time the Sherwoods lost 1,520 men. The Derbyshire Regiment suffered similar casualties, many in the Far East. These and other lives lost at sea and in the skies must be remembered in gratitude for their sacrifice and as a warning to us. Lest we forget.

What a busy place this was. St Peter's Street was crowded to overflowing. Pedestrians had to step into the street to make any progress. The traffic was not faring much better. It was a slow procession that made its way past Millett's and Thurman and Malin's. The latter was a fine department store. It sold a huge range of quality products that would have been envied on London's Bond Street. The founders were Harry Thurman and William Malin. They had been employees at George and George, the specialists in silk and woollens. They found themselves out of work in the mid 1870s when the company closed. Undaunted, Thurman and Malin opened their own store. The four storey building had an attractive and highly polished bronze frontage. Its

first customers came through the door in 1879. As the venture grew in success, so the premises expanded to include St Peter's churchyard. It was one of the first department stores to introduce an electric lift for the benefit of its customers. Despite its excellent reputation Thurman and Malin's store did not reach its centenary. It closed in July 1970. The variety of traffic passing by its front door in this image illustrated the great divide in social class that could be accommodated within Derby. Just yards apart were a magnificent Rolls Royce and a humble motor cycle and sidecar. The rider of the bike preferred a cap to a proper helmet for his protection. The decision would be taken out of his hands when legislation was passed that made it illegal to dispense with a crash helmet.

On the move

Above: The bus station on Morledge was a fine example of old meeting the modern. The vehicles look like little dinky cars and have a truly period feel. In contrast, the up to date lines of the bus station complex lend a sense of the futuristic to this photograph. It was taken in May 1933. Building work had begun in October 1932, using local brick. It was only right that it should have a modern and forward looking appearance. The age of the tram had almost passed and the time of the motor bus had fully arrived. This station was not just a place to hop on a bus. It had other facilities for passengers not to be found in railway stations. As well as the usual offices, there was a chemist, a delightful café and spacious waiting rooms. The platform layout provided simple access to the buses and was one of the first of its kind in the country. The official opening took place on 2 October 1933, just 12 months after the building work had begun. That it was open for business before that date was a credit to the builders. In those inter war years Derby was a market town. The bus station provided a vital connection with the outlying districts. People were glad of a quick and comfortable service that could bring them into the heart of the town to shop and do business. In 1973 a bridge was built to link it to the Eagle Centre. However, that was demolished when the multi storey car park at the Cockpit was erected.

Bottom: Are these two about to start some form of 1933 road rage? The two cyclists seem to be staring each other down. Perhaps the one on the left was some form of pedal pushing boy racer who has just cut up the chap in the collar and tie. Notice how his bikeclips make his trousers seem to billow out above his ankles. He had no chain guard on his machine and it would have been easy for him to get oil on his turnups or snag the material in the chain. Bicycles were sturdy and reliable machines and everyone owned one. It was not unusual to see businessmen riding into work. However, the bus was the favoured way for the public to travel. Trams would soon disappear and the new bus station that had just opened was choc a block with passengers. The Trent bus on the right is off to Swadlincote, passing through Melbourne and Hartshorne on the way. Crossing in the centre of the picture are two men wearing the flat cap that was the symbol of the working class. The women near to them are probably a cut above. One is sporting a fur collar that was very warm and very chic. If it were real fur she would be told off these days. The pram at their side was a chunky affair. Baby was kept solidly safe in this carriage. After all, it had to be sturdy. It might be used to carry coal or the weekly shopping when its passenger was old enough to toddle.

Right: The Rolls Royce on the left had its spare wheel mounted on the side with a running board underneath it. That prewar style of car always brings to mind the days of Chicago gangsters and Eliot Ness' Untouchables. Films and newsreels of the era showed us American hoods spraying machine bullets around from just such a type of car. However, to suggest that this pictured motor might have been

involved in some form of Midlands' Mafia is stretching things just too far! The Cornmarket has seen some lively moments, but Michigan Avenue it is not. St Peter's Street stretches away in front of Burton's tailors. The SOS 1939 single decker Derby Corporation bus had an emergency method of starting its engine. As with most vehicles those days it had a starting handle. In cold or damp weather an engine was notoriously difficult to start. Pulling the starter switch on the dashboard did not always turn over the engine sufficiently to get it going. If not, it was time for the starting handle. Placed in the slot at the front, it was hand cranked to try to get the engine going. It was usually a two person job. Many a little child became adept at pumping the accelerator pedal while dad was huffing and puffing away at the front. It was a doubly difficult job to see to an engine of the size that was fitted to a bus. That did take some effort. The handle sticking out through the bus radiator would not be allowed these days. It was a frightful hazard in an accident.

buses in service had topped 100. Roe built the last buses to be bought in 1960. By 1963 it was announced that they would be phased out in favour of diesel engined transport. The overhead gantries and cables were in danger of falling down. The system needed overhaul or replacement. The last pantograph sucked electricity from the cables in 1967 as the 224 made its final journey.

Top: The sleek black lines of the Derby registered Wolseley saloon caught admiring glances along Babington Lane in the summer of 1964. It was one of the finest British cars ever to leave Herbert Austin's Longbridge plant. The very first 1895 model was a three wheeler. He did not add the extra wheel until 1900. The motor cyclist behind was covering all options. He was displaying badges for both the AA and RAC. Once upon a time riders who worked for either breakdown company used to salute fellow members as they passed by. That little bit of old world courtesy was done away with when petty officials said that it was an unsafe practice. The trolley buses, once described as trackless trams, were full of passengers as they passed Stevens' men's outfitter. St Peter's Church was in view behind the motor bike. The young man looking towards the Wolseley was dressed in a suit. Casual wear around town was the exception. His hairstyle still favoured that of the late 1950s, with its quiff and slick backed sides. The longer mophead style favoured by the Beatles was only just beginning to catch on. This fellow looked more like Billy Fury, after Cliff Richard, Britain's top male singer of the era. Ronald Wycherley, to give Billy his real name, was in the charts from 1959 to 1983, the year of his untimely death from heart failure at the age of 41. His last hit was 'Forget Him'. This pedestrian would not have done.

Above: Trolley buses were able to make some use of the old tramway system. Although the overhead cabling had to be altered, many of the supports and stanchions could be recycled. When these buses were pressed into service, in 1932, it was not as expensive as starting from new. They sounded the death knell for the trams that only lived side by side with the new form of public transport for another two years. The big six wheeler, diesel engined 47 horse power omnibus that Michael Flanders and Donald Swann used to sing about was to come later. Outside Midland Station, we are looking at no 117 electric trolley bus, a Guy BTX Brush three axled, 75 horsepower model. Rees Roturbo provided its electrical equipment. The first journey undertaken by trolley buses was along Nottingham Road to the cemetery. Perhaps they were going there to pay their last respects to the trams. They were sturdy, reliable machines. The inaugural fleet was not replaced until 1949. That coincided with the Corporation Transport's golden jubilee. By that date the number of trolley

Above: What was the price of a gallon of petrol in 1958? A few bob, perhaps? Compare that with 21st century prices that have soared so much that the counters on pumps are struggling to cope with recording such high prices. New calibrations on the pumps will push the price up even further. This Esso filling station was at the junction of Ashbourne Road and Kingsway. Esso was really Standard Oil, but the initials of the company gave the firm its new and snappier name. The woman filling the car belonged to a breed of forecourt attendants who did the lot. They filled the tank, wiped the windscreen and even checked the oil if you wanted them to. Having accepted your money, they were the ones who operated the till as well. Now it is all self service. Are you going to meet the boyfriend, dressed in your best gear? If you need to fill up on the way,

hard luck. Do it yourself and arrive at the restaurant smelling of diesel. 'Nice perfume, love' is not the best way to start the evening. The little pumps, dishing out Premium and Regular, might look antiquated to the modern eye. We have got used to the multi grade dispenser. We now have unleaded, lead replacement petrol and diesel for our tanks. The engines run more smoothly and they are so much more reliable. Inside we have stereo systems, CD players, heated screens and air conditioning. There is only one problem. We cannot afford to put in any juice!

Above right: This is the garage workshop that was later to become Kenning's. In the 1930s it belonged to GS Oscroft and Co Ltd. It was a company of motor engineers on Derwent Street. The garage looked more like an aircraft hangar. It was a huge enterprise. The stores department ran to three decks and it held a vast range of spare parts. Cars were not as reliable

as they are today. Spare parts were in constant demand as breakdowns were frequent. Oscroft's handled the distribution throughout the county for Vauxhall and Bedford Motors. The company prided itself on being able to get large quantities of work coming in. Its ambition was then to turn jobs round quickly. Not surprisingly, it had the motto 'get 'em in, get 'em out'. The garage also ran a valeting service. Customers were charged according to their cars' engine sizes. The price board showed that a car in the 9-12 horsepower range would be rated at 8s 9d. That is about 44p in today's money. Judging by the line of cars waiting to be serviced, it was a garage that was kept very busy. Many of these vehicles would have to be put into mothballs when the war came. Petrol rationing meant that motoring was only for essential journeys. The rise in popularity of car travel in the 1930s went on hold until the 1950s. When the brakes of rationing came off, the accelerator of car ownership was pressed once more.

Back in England in 1970, following swift negotiations, the company then known as Autofair became only the third Mercedes-Benz commercial dealer in Britain, opening its doors for business in Burton on Trent on 3rd January 1971. £15,000 was scraped together to get the new business off the ground, it was a great deal of money then - but the fear and excitement which such a personal commitment generated would be more than justified with sales which would eventually exceed £30 million a year; although that degree of success was still many years in the future.

Starting a new business from scratch is never easy but Don Marshall's team gave it everything. At a time when demonstrators were almost unheard of in the truck business there was hardly a day when Autofair's 32 ton LPS1418 truck was not out on the road being shown to potential customers.

The very first truck order came from Eric Skeet of Draycott Transport in Burton. At a cost of £6,250 it was no small investment for Draycotts, but it was to become the first of several Mercedes to join their fleet in subsequent years.

The year 1971 proved an eventful one. Interest grew as the months progressed and Bert Deacon was pleased to report to the company board at the year end that Don Marshall and his team had sold over 70 vehicles. 'We'll double that next year' he said. And they did.

In 1971 Mercedes-Benz commercial vehicles were still relatively rare on Britain's roads. The name

meant prestige cars to most people who thought of its motor racing heritage, luxury limousines and beautiful convertibles. Yet the firm of Mercedes-Benz, or rather its predecessors, had in fact been building trucks since the end of the 19th century. Mercedes-Benz's profile in the UK commercial vehicle sector was remarkably low despite Britain being the largest commercial vehicle market in Europe. Not that the name was unknown amongst those professional truck drivers who drove to the continent; they had seen Mercedes trucks driven by foreign colleagues and had stopped to admire them at transport stops all across Europe. Many of those drivers had commented to their haulage company owners what fine vehicles the Germans were producing, and asked the question - why can't I have a 'Merc' to drive too.

The 1970s changed the situation dramatically. Autofair was amongst the first of several new franchises to be awarded in the first half of the decade and as the popularity of the marque grew Daimler-Benz, the owners of the name, formed a new British subsidiary Mercedes-Benz (UK) in 1974.

The seventies saw a revolution in commercial vehicle design with the disappearance of the old bull-nose tractor units to be replaced by sleeker vehicles such as the mould-breaking T1 light transporter range.

Above: *The first stretch limo sold by the company - a 1982 Mercedes-Benz 240.*

Other developments at Mercedes-Benz during this period included the introduction of a new generation of cab and the launch of a full range of 'Vee' formation engines making the company the first manufacturer to successfully introduce that configuration of power plant into commercial vehicles.

Customers who tried out one Mercedes truck found themselves coming back again and again: Dave Shilton has now been using Mertrux vehicles for almost thirty years, Mick Clark of MD Clark has similarly bought vehicles for more than two decades as have Allegro Transport, Anthony & Spencer, Putzmeister, FP Walker Limited. Trent Insulations, Courtaulds Chemicals and Frank Wright of Ashbourne. All have dealt with Mertrux for a number of years.

Central to Mertrux's success has been the people who have worked for the firm. Several worked with Bert Deacon and Don

Marshall, in their pre-Mercedes days and would come to be regarded as 'lifers' with the firm. Keith Godfrey for example Parts Manager since 1982 had been with Bert and Don since he was an apprentice mechanic in 1962. Truck Workshop Foreman Chris Insley began as an apprentice mechanic in 1967

Above: *The demonstration of a truck to the country's first lady HGV driver - Val Sutton.* **Below:** *Mr Lloyd with the first car sold by the company...and his replacement.*

whilst amongst the firm's fitters Rod Stringer joined the firm in 1973 and Paul Carey in 1975. The team would come to rank as one of the most experienced in the Mercedes truck dealership network.

Another 'old-timer' would be Martin Stock who became a van and truck salesman in 1977 and would eventually become Mertrux's Commercial Vehicle Sales Director. In 1978 Ian Jones became known as 'six' because he was the sixth person to join the parts department; he had been helping his father John Jones on Saturday morning for years - John Jones had actually joined Bert Deacon in 1936 and was Mertrux Parts Manager until his retirement in 1982.

Other 'life termers' would come to include Simon Whitaker who joined the parts department in 1974 and Truck Service Advisor Robert Yates who joined in 1978 along with Ruth Brobyn who would become Don Marshall's secretary.

Bert Deacon formally retired from Mertrux in 1978 although he retained a formal role as chairman of the holding company.

In 1981 Mercedes Benz offered Autofair the passenger car franchise for Derby. This was a tribute to the success and professionalism of the commercial vehicle operation - and an extra cause for celebration in the firm's 10th anniversary year.

A bigger business called for larger premises and so on 1st September 1981 the whole organisation relocated from Burton to Chequers Road, Pentagon Island in Derby. And with that move came a change of name to Mertrux (Derby) Ltd. (it was to have been Mertrucks but an inspiration by Don Marshall's wife Hazel whilst travelling on the M1 had led to 'trucks' becoming 'trux').

The new premises cost half a million pounds and consisted of 6,000 sq ft of showrooms, 9,000 sq ft of workshops and a 3,000 sq ft parts department with meticulously planned and equipped offices and car park.

With the diversification into passenger cars it was agreed to recruit a sales manager to head up the new division. In September 1981 Norman Smith walked into a showroom with no lights, no carpet no customers... and a stubbed finger. Norman had been involved in selling cars and motor cycles since the 1960s. Norman remembered his job interview well, not least because at its conclusion Don Marshall presented him with a gift for his two children - a Charles and Diana engagement rug!

The year 1981 was one of recession in the British economy yet despite that the Derby franchise still managed to sell its full quota of 80 vehicles, and for the first time achieved a turnover of £2 million.

The first passenger car sale was for a 200 Auto in champagne with light brown leather. It was bought by a Mr Lloyd of Derby at a cost of £9,000 and was run by him without fault for ten years before being part exchanged in 1991. The car is now owned by Mertrux and carefully preserved. The first car to actually be delivered to a customer however was a 280E which went to another local businessman, Kevin Ellis, who has remained a loyal customer ever since.

Two years after beginning selling cars another long serving employee who joined the car division was Jon Rolley who would eventually become car workshop manager.

Above: *Two early advertising campaigns.*

The 1980s were a period for celebration for Mertrux; not only were sales buoyant but staff were making enormous contribution to the firm's reputation. In 1983 Keith Godfrey's sterling performance in the parts department was nationally recognised by Mercedes-Benz with the award of Parts Manager of the Year. In 1987 Norman Smith made the intellectual limelight as a finalist in the Pan-European Product Masters competition - a Mastermind -style quiz based on Mercedes product knowledge - Norman spent two days in Berlin and even got to sit in the real Mastermind chair.

As the business continued to grow it became clear that the premises were not large enough and in 1987 work began on a new five-acre site just a few hundred yards from Pentagon Island on West Meadows Industrial Estate. In true Marshall style the deal was done in two days and the building was up in just five months.

The 1980s were to prove an important decade for Mercedes-Benz. The greatest development was the introduction of the compact car in 1983. With the launch of the 190 model Mercedes opened up a mass car market for the first time and in the process brought the prestige and quality of one of the world's greatest marques within the price range of a whole new customer group. This helped lift Mercedes-Benz car sales in the UK up from 13,000 to over 23,000 in the following five years.

In 1987 the 200 series was launched to replace the hardy 123 and brought a new streamlining to Mercedes car design - adopting a more rounded softer look. Amongst the car's innovations was multi link rear suspension.

Finally the decade saw the rebirth of the legendary SL, the ultimate grand tourer. For Mertrux and the rest of the dealer network there was an exhilarating two days in Spain putting the vehicle through its mind blowing paces on the Circuito de Jerez. The new SL,

Above: *A long service presentation to Dave Allen, used commercial sales director (left) who had served 25 years with the firm, at one of the company's Christmas parties by Danny La Rue. Don Marshall is on the right.* **Below:** *The Dealer of the Year Award 1995.*

beauty aside, was to be the first of a new generation of hi-tech computer controlled cars: its hood mechanism alone boasted 13 different electronic functions.

Meanwhile on the commercial vehicle front there had been a number of important developments in the 1980s starting with the 7.5 tonne 814 which became International Truck of the year in 1984 scoring the highest marks awarded in its then nine year history winning the votes of all 13 international judges.

The year 1986 saw the introduction of Mercedes-Benz Powerliners the most powerful trucks yet to sport the famous three pointed star. The top of the range 1644S was the first to exceed the 400 bhp threshold. The Powerliner was a landmark vehicle featuring as standard the EPS gearbox which

brought a new relaxed driving to Britain's truck drivers.

The decade of the eighties saw two important corporate developments for Mercedes-Benz UK. The move to a new 35 acre headquarters in Tongwell, Milton Keynes in 1984 and the 1987 opening of a new 78 acre commercial vehicle preparation site at Wentworth Park near Barnsley, a site still regarded with the envy throughout the truck industry.

By the 1990s Mertrux had matured as a business, reaping the benefits of the care an patience put into it from its birth. The decade began with a commitment by the company to achieving the rigorous quality standards required by ISO 9002: the painstaking programme was completed in just under six months and the company became the first Mercedes-Benz dealership in the UK to receive certification.

The 1990s was another decade full of awards. Martin Stock was chosen by Mercedes-Benz for the prestigious title of Truck Sales Manager of the year in 1990. That success was followed two years later with John Deakin winning the Accountant of the Year Award.

Left: *The showroom in 1981.*
Top: *Derby County Show - 1982.*

1993 saw a bumper crop of awards with Martin Stock again becoming Truck Sales Manager of the Year and the company being chosen from all the franchises in the UK to be acclaimed Truck Dealer of the Year. The occasion was marked by Mertrux hosting a tour of the Crown Derby factory and a Mercedes-Benz dinner for all winners at the Priest House Hotel in Castle Donington. It was appropriate that the same year saw Mercedes seize a 10 per cent share of the UK commercial vehicle market with sales of over 12,000 vans and trucks.

In its Silver Jubilee year Mertrux was again celebrating a triumph being awarded National Truck Dealer of the Year for the second time in three years.

The 1993 launch of the 'C' class brought the compact car into a new era. More and more people grew to appreciate the benefits of owning a 'Merc' not least because its famed residual value.

The launch of the 'E' class in 1995 represented another landmark in Mercedes design evolution - the vehicle's distinctive appearance reflecting a more youthful, avant-garde approach.

The addition of the SLK coupe 'C' and 'E' class estates and 'V' class people carrier were important extensions of the range but the biggest revolution came in 1998 with the launch of the 'A' class, the ultimate supermini. The first ever Mercedes small

Above: The 1995 Derby County Show.
Right: Sponsorship of the local children's football team, the Etwall Comets.

car moved the company into the mass market in the widest sense providing it with a product for every market sector.

With the appointment to the board in 1994 of Martin Stock, Norman Smith and Joe O'Reilly the company recognised the invaluable contribution of its senior team members.

In 1996, to mark 25 years in business, Mertrux' long-standing customers were invited to a celebratory dinner attended by Stirling Moss which was held at Donington Park amidst the world's largest collection of Grand Prix Racing cars. During that silver jubilee year Mertrux shared its success with others, donating a battery powered child sized Jeep to Derby's Children's Hospital as well as sponsoring the local children's football team the Etwall

customers as Don Marshall has had the company can look forward to celebrating a very enjoyable Golden Jubilee in 2021 selling and maintaining the ever-more impressive range of Mercedes vehicles to ever-more satisfied customers.

Comets and raising money to buy ambulances and a Derby community bus for under privileged children.

Mertrux is now the longest established Mercedes truck dealership in the country and one of the top performers. Its passenger car franchise has enjoyed continuous growth since it began. This growth led to the opening of two further branches in Nottingham and Leicester in 1998, making Mertrux the main Mercedes-Benz dealership in the East Midlands.

A new generation of younger managers is now coming through the ranks and all four of Don Marshall's children, Ian, Sarah, Judith and Matthew have connections with the business: Ian Marshall is dealer principal, having begun his career with the company 17 years ago whilst his brother Matthew is marketing manager. Matthew began in 1994 at the very bottom of the career ladder, valeting and cleaning cars. Team development is being pursued through the achievement of the nationally recognised Investors in People Award. And if one lesson can be learned from Don Marshall, and the remarkable success the Mertrux business has enjoyed over three decades, it is that it is people; staff, customers and suppliers, who make a successful business just as much as the effort and initiative of its founders.

If the next generation of Mertrux managers enjoy the same degree of loyalty and support from staff and

By the opening year of the 21st century Mertrux had succeeded in helping make Mercedes-Benz one of the most popular cars in Britain and also had changed the face of commercial traffic on Britain's Roads. When Mertrux set out in business three decades earlier Mercedes trucks were virtually unknown in Britain, today whilst the sight of a Mercedes truck may be commonplace, thanks to Mertrux and its dedicated team their reputation for quality remains undiluted. As the company embarks on the new millennium, Don Marshall would like to thank everyone involved in its success, and apologise to anyone whose name has not been mentioned in this feature!

Above left: *The workshop in 1995.*
Above right: *The Dealer of the Year Award 1993.*
Below: *The Chequers Road showroom today.*

At the shops

Central Education Ltd, St Peter's Street in 1938 was a treasure trove of all the equipment a student needed to get through the academic year. The ground floor showroom, seen in 1938, held a host of pens, papers, cases and books that were a must for a day in the classroom. The busiest time was always August. That was the month for youngsters to be dragged round the clothes stores for cream blouses, gym slips, pleated skirts, white socks, sensible shoes and a blazer and tie in the school colours. As one wag said, 'That was only the boys!' Having been hauled round the various tailors and outfitters, there was at least some choice when they got into the Central Education store. The better off went to the display cabinet of Parker and Waterman fountain pens. Lazlo Biro had just brought out his

ballpoint pen, but they were still regarded as too common for use in proper schools. Inky fingers and blotting paper were the signs of a decent education. In this store children got their pencil cases and filled them with a rubber, pencil sharpener, little ruler, compasses and a template for drawing circles and triangles. School satchels were bought and loaded with notebooks and sketchpads. Cumberland and Lakeland coloured pencils were added to the pile and the children were nearly ready to face the first day back at school. All that remained was to sew name tags into all the clothing and stencil names onto the other equipment. Then they were ready to sit in rows of seats and desks facing the blackboard and use their rulers to fire bits of paper dipped in the inkwell across the classroom when 'miss' turned her back.

This imposing building, designed by Albert Bromley, was erected in 1912 on the corner of St Peter's Street and East Street. Jesse Boot, later Lord Trent, opened the first of his many shops in Nottingham in 1877. His father had an interest in country potions and remedies that Jesse inherited. He experimented with all manner of combinations of herbs that he turned into patent medicines. Boots' shops, though, concentrated on more established lines as Jesse opened other stores in Lincoln, Sheffield and this one in our town. Extensions were made to the building in 1938 along East Street. Of particular interest were the four statues in niches spaced above the shop frontage. They were sculpted by Morley Harder and represent four notable Derby figures. Florence Nightingale lived much of her early life in the county before achieving fame as the 'Lady of the Lamp' at the Barrack Hospital, Scutari in the Crimean War. She was the first woman to receive the Order of Merit and lived to the ripe old age of 90. John Lombe was a member of the family that established the Silk Mill and turned a once cottage industry into a thriving business. William Hutton was born in Full Street in 1723. After working in the Silk Mill, he became a bookseller. He collected historical information and published a history of Derby in 1791. The fourth figure is of Jedediah Strutt. Born in 1726, he was the first of the family of mill owners and public benefactors. Halifax Building Society took over these premises in 1975.

arks and Spencer Ltd came in for some battering as the 20th century drew to a close. It was criticised for not moving with the times, but was making attempts to modernise in the first years of the new millennium. It was the reliability and quality of its clothing that had built the chain store's reputation. You could trust 'Marks and Sparks'. This branch opened on 19 May 1933 on the corner of Thorntree Lane and St Peter's Street, next to the Irish Linen Company. The building was purchased from the Prudential. The assurance company retained offices on the top floor until 1960 when the store extended its sales area. Earlier alterations had taken place in 1940. The store had only been open for about two years when this photograph was taken. It had already become one of Derby's premier stores. Marks and Spencer became one of the few places where men were comfortable in shopping for presents for their wives or girlfriends. The famous St Michael brand name was a promise of sensible clothing. As long as he knew her size, a man could buy the missus a blouse or cardigan without embarrassment. The more daring could even sneak something up to the counter from the lingerie area. Department stores in those days often had tubes of money whizzing through the air on a form of monorail on their way to the cashier. The change then came flying back to the shop assistant. Even at Marks it is all credit cards now.

Above: In 1928 Britain was celebrating that a decade had passed since the first world war ended. It was a time of mixed fortune. America had the limits of prohibition whilst women were becoming more free in the way they dressed and behaved. They could even vote. Their hair was more boyish and skirts grew shorter. Officialdom was shocked. The Germans banned government employees from the wearing of hemlines less than eight inches below the knee. All this while Amelia Earhart was flying the Atlantic. At home, more and more motor cars were appearing on the roads. Traffic accidents rose alarmingly. There was no driving test until the mid 1930s. The Derby Vulcanising Company tried to do its bit for road safety. This Trent charabanc was part of an advertising campaign for the company's tyres. Vulcanisation is a chemical process that gives rubber higher strength and resistance to swelling and abrasion. As it made tyres more elastic over a greater range of temperatures, it helped make road holding easier. The hoardings behind the 'chara' were filled with adverts of the day for everything from Camp coffee to the twice nightly show at the Grand, featuring the London Players in 'If Four Walls Told'. The Daily Sketch was a popular tabloid that had been begun in Manchester in 1909 by Sir Edward Hulton. One advert reminds some of the story about the child who slipped on a bar of soap. That's life - buoy!

The name of Cockpit Hill gives you some idea of the cruel and barbaric sport that used to take place there. It was popular with all social classes and flourished even into the 19th century. The photographer of this 1932 scene was standing on the spot where people used to gamble on the outcome of contests between pairs of gamecocks that had specially sharpened metal spurs fitted to their feet. Down below is a good view of the old Morledge Market. It was one of the foremost of its type in the country. A constant babble of talk at banter echoed around the stalls as traders encouraged housewives to part with their housekeeping money. They were careful with their cash. These were the days when unemployment was high and wages were held down.

Feelings ran high. In London's Trafalgar Square thousands attended rallies and demonstrations held against the policies of Ramsay MacDonald's government. At Morledge carts and lorries that had brought produce from outlying districts stood on the waste land behind the market. Those traders who could not afford covered pitches spread their wares on tables or on the ground. They seem to have attracted the interest of men in whatever they had for sale. The more practical women were searching the main market for bargains to help them stretch the family budget a little further. In the distance you can make out the distinctive shapes of the Guildhall, All Saints, St Alkmund's, St Mary's and the power station. The old silk mill can be seen down by the river Derwent.

Below: It is 3.05 on the illuminated clock of the fourth Guildhall building to have stood on this site, overlooking Market Place. The Guildhall belltower stands 112 feet above the ground. In the distance, the tower of St Peter's Church can be seen. The market was in full swing on this day. By the early 1900s, when this picture was taken, trams were carrying passengers to the place that had been serving local citizens for nearly 700 years. In 1229 the burgesses were allowed to hold a market in the town. At first, permission was only granted for the sale of cloth. This was to be the forerunner that reflected the great cloth industry that sprang up in medieval times and developed into a thriving cottage industry. By the 18th century, threads, woven and dyed cloth and stockings were much in evidence. Italian silk came to Derby around this time and the first ever industrial mill in Britain was built in Derby. The market expanded from just cloth to other produce and, around 1330, another market appeared on Friargate. Fixed stalls in the Great Market were passed down through the family and other markets sprang up around the centre. Many of the nearby place names, such as Irongate and Sadlergate, show the sort of business these markets conducted. There were also coopers, goldsmiths and glove makers selling their wares. A moot hall (council hall) was built in Market Place and it had its own court from 1446. It could collect its own fines and this all added to the wealth of the area. At the far end of the stalls there is a statue of the Liberal MP and 19th century town benefactor, Michael Thomas Bass.

Bottom: On the right dad has been relegated to the role of baby minder. His child sits happily whilst the so-called head of the family plays second fiddle to the missus. This is shopping after all. A man knew his place in that scheme of things. It was the housewife who handled the housekeeping money and decided what was on the menu for the week's meals. She had her favourite stalls in Morledge Market. However, an eye for a bargain never prevented her from

changing allegiance. It was up to the silver tongue of the stallholder to convince her that his wares were the best value for money. There were plenty of characters who tried their best to get customers to open their purses. One of the fondest memories shoppers brought to mind was of Mad Harry. He had one of the wittiest and quickest lines in patter of any of the stallholders. His rapid fire style of auction selling, at what he called ridiculous prices, was the reason for his nickname. Morledge had plenty of space for shoppers to move along the aisles between the stalls. It was just as well because it was a popular and busy place. The market was replaced by the Law Courts and moved its business to the Eagle Centre.

Below centre: Derby's Drill Hall has echoed to marching feet as ranks of soldiers were put through their paces. More often than not, the hall would echo to the sound of other feet. The public often came in to view the various promotions and displays that it held. This was a promotion stand that was trying to encourage a new generation of newspaper readers. Parents were being encouraged to buy the Junior Mirror for their kids by appealing to their patriotism. War stories and tales of remarkable dogs were the ways that the Mirror used to try to get a new readership in tow. Children's comics used similar stories to attract a clientele. There was 'I flew with Braddock', all about a brave RAF ace. Lassie and Rin Tin Tin were popular canine characters performing remarkable feats of skill and bravery. Amazing sporting performances by the indestructible ageless Wilson and the soccer playing genius of Limp-along Leslie fascinated the reader. Girls reached for Girls' Crystal and School Friend. Those who had no clue what a dormitory was still marvelled at the hooded adventures of the Secret Three. The Mirror was right to try to woo youngsters to the Junior paper. In those days reading was a popular way to spend your time. Modern youth would not know a library or news stand if it fell over them. It was a pity, though, that the Mirror stand was also promoting Wills' tobacco and Kensitas cigarettes. Some example!

Bottom: In a little shop on Toad Lane, Rochdale a small acorn was planted. It grew into the Co-operative Society. In 1844, a group of businessmen pooled their resources to sell goods to the working classes at favourable prices. Customers were made members and shared in the profits. Tokens and stamps towards a dividend, or 'divi', were collected and exchanged at the Co-op for cash or discounted goods. Some profits were set aside to support the education of the poor. The co-operative movement developed rapidly in the latter part of the 19th century, particularly in the industrial and mining areas of northern England and Scotland. In Derby, Jonathan Henderson, the secretary of the Carpenters and Joiners Association, heard about the experiment in the east Lancashire town. In 1849 he wrote for information to the Rochdale pioneers of the co-operative movement. With the help of a dozen Association colleagues and just £2 as starting capital, Jonathan started the Derby Co-operative Society. It was only Britain's second co-op. In small premises in a yard off Sadlergate, operating just three nights a week, the venture proved popular. By 1857 Derby Co-op moved to two rooms on Victoria Street. Sales were now up to £10 per week. At first membership was limited to Association and union members, but in 1859 sales were made to the general public. The store in this nighttime photograph was opened in 1871. It stood on the corner of Albert Street and Exchange Street.

The trolley bus was coming away from The Spot in 1948, travelling along St Peter's Street. It was doing the run in and out of Allestree. No one is really sure how The Spot came to get its name. It is generally accepted that first reference to it was made in the 1740s when a reporter on the Derby Weekly Mercury used the term. What caused him to use that description, we do not know. But, the name stuck. The Wolseley car was leading the way past crowded pavements. They were times of narrow streets, by comparison with today. The rising population overflowed all too easily into the road and accidents were commonplace. As car ownership grew, the road safety and traffic congestion problem concerned us all. The year the photograph was taken was memorable for a number of reasons. On the sporting field we said goodbye to the world's best ever batsman. Australia's Don Bradman bowed out with a score that was out of the ordinary for him. He was bowled by Eric Hollies for a duck! Matt Busby managed Manchester United to the FA Cup, the first of his many successes. London hosted the Olympic Games. They were graced by Emil Zatopek and Fanny Blankers-Koen, athletes who became household names. Freddie Mills became world light heavyweight boxing champion. Elsewhere the Berlin airlift got under way. Mahatma Ghandi was murdered in New Delhi, the state of Israel was born and the Japanese wartime leader, General Tojo, was hanged for war crimes. Perhaps the event with the biggest impact for all of us in Britain was the formation of the National Health Service.

homas Potter Townsend was the 'oil and colour man' of Sadlergate Bridge. On this packed stand in the Drill Hall was everything you might need to keep the home polished, painted and shining clean. One product being heavily promoted was Brushing Belco. It made things bright and beautiful and dried in an hour, or so it claimed. It could paint everything from a pram to a lamp standard. There was black lead and polish for fire grates and kitchen ranges. In the 1930s many homes still had meals cooked on large coal fired ranges that heated the room as well. Kettles were put on hobs and irons warmed up ready to tackle the ironing. Stews bubbled on top while bread was baked in the oven. The black ranges were leaded and kept sparkling by housewives who took a pride in their kitchens. Copper pans hung off the wall and her skill as a homemaker was seldom in doubt, just as long as hubby tipped up his pay packet each week. Townsend also provided some aids for the handyman. Plastic wood was modern product that helped patch up chips and holes that were difficult to fill in. The stone jars, either side of the ornate wrought iron table legs, have now become collectors' items at antique fairs. In the 1930s, before the days of refrigerators, they were sturdy vessels that could keep dangerous liquids safe. They were also nice and cool storage jars for putting in the larder.

wall mounted hot water geyser. This little boiler provided almost instant hot water. For the housewife, this was a great help, although it only produced a small quantity of water before it needed reheating. A lot of homes had to heat up water for washing and bathing in kettles and pans on the kitchen range. Not everyone had a back boiler.

Top: The Drill Hall on Newland Street, just off Abbey Street, often held trade fairs. Its spacious hall was a favourite place to hold a promotion. In 1935 it was the turn of Dalton's. All the radiograms, wirelesses and record players of the day were on show. Second from the left on the front row is a Murphy A26 radio. Families clustered around the radio in the evenings, listening to the news and the light enter-

Above: The wonder of modern electrical aids to those washday blues was being recommended to us by Beatty Bros. This trade display in the Drill Hall was intended to encourage visitors to go to Beatty's shop and invest in the latest in modern technology. Quite what 21st century trading standards officers would make of the claim on the right is open to argument. 'Electricity saves more than it costs' is a statement of doubtful accuracy! Beatty Bros Ltd was not just a retail outlet, it also produced its own machines. The display looks like something out of a museum to those of us for whom Monday is just another day. Microchips, integrated and programmable circuit boards and powerful motors have revolutionised laundry day. In the 1930s electrical appliances were a new concept still out of reach of most of the working class. Many people still used dolly tubs, hand cranked mangles and a washing line. These first electric washers and driers were, for them, just a pipe dream. But, the revolution had to begin somewhere. At the back of the display is a small

tainment programmes. They spent their sixpence to get a copy of the 'Radio Times' and planned out the listening. 'Red sails in the sunset', 'Blue Moon' and 'Smoke gets in your eyes' were among the memorable songs of the year. They were tunes and lyrics that are still popular today. Who can say that anyone will bother to sing the Corrs' 'Breathless' or anything recorded by Snoop Doggy Dogg in years to come? We had Gracie Fields to listen to, Henry Hall's orchestra to send us dreamy or Benny Goodman to swing to. Music was played on records (remember them?) that spun at 78 revolutions per minute. Long playing records were still 15 years away. The promotion window had adverts for Columbia records. That was the label on which the Peter Pan of pop music, Sir Cliff Richard, would release the first of his 125 hit records. However, the most famous recording sight is the one on the HMV record label. His Master's Voice was immediately recognisable because of Nipper, the dog. Whoever thought up that masterpiece of a logo was a genius.

In Morledge Market there was a vast array of fresh produce for sale. Rows of shiny Cox's Pippins vied with the rich colours of Victoria plums. They stacked them high without a single polythene wrapper or polystyrene tray in sight. Oranges were carried in boxes that little boys could cadge and turn into a set of cricket stumps in the street that same evening. Vegetables retailed at so many pennies and shillings to the pound. Stallholders shouted the price in pounds and ounces without the fear of some petty official from the trading standards people telling them it had to be kilos and grams. No-one confiscated weighing scales because they only displayed imperial measures. Housewives did not care about metrication. They knew about quality and value. That was why they came to the market and why they cannot be fussed with 300 millilitres of this and 400 cc of that even today. This market was part of the central improvement scheme. As the bus station was close by it was convenient for shoppers to come in from the outlying districts. Opening in 1933, there were 240 stalls, all under cover but it still retained the feel of the traditional open market. The cries of the vendors and their merry quips with their customers were all part of a day's shopping. It was a place of entertainment as well as commerce. The site is now home to the new courthouse. The market moved to the Eagle Centre in 1975 and lost a lot of its charm and atmosphere in doing so.

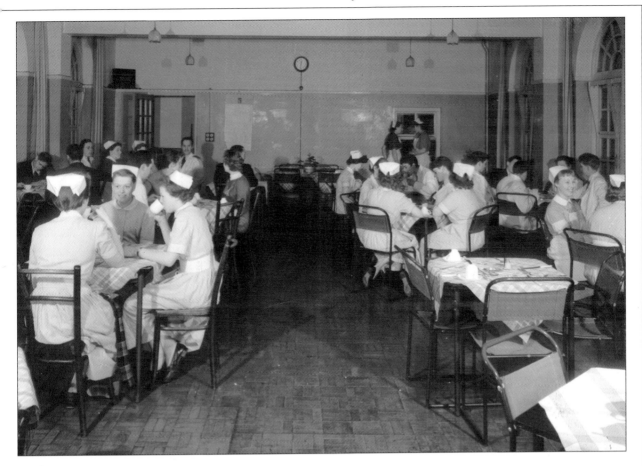

Making a living

In Victorian times they called a spade a definite shovel! There was little political correctness about some of the descriptions used for its institutions. This was part of Derby County Lunatic Asylum to the west of the city at Mickleover. That did not mean a place where football fanatics were locked up, but what came to be known as a mental hospital. When it was built in 1848 it did not just incarcerate the mentally ill. Teenage single mothers, epileptics and others who were an embarrassment to their families were shut away. This sort of practice, on a smaller scale, was still happening well into the 20th century. The building was a delightful piece of Elizabethan style of architecture, designed by Henry Duesbury. The front of the asylum was faced with the red brick fired from the estate's red clay. The first patient was admitted in 1851. It was a mixed establishment with room for 300 men and women. A chapel and further wards were added in 1869 and 1874. It opened its own farm in the grounds in 1911. Milk and produce from it was used to supply the hospital, as it had now become known. From its unfortunate Victorian connections, it had developed to become the well respected Pastures Hospital. The dedicated nurses seen in the staff canteen were a far cry from the harridans who patrolled the corridors and wards of the old asylum, deaf to the cries of the wretches it held. The hospital closed in 1993 and a residential estate was built on its memories.

At Long Eaton, in the southeast of Derbyshire, the Pressacts company made electrical parts for Power Samos. These, and the printed circuitry it manufactured, went into the gadgetry that ran our cars. The machinery looks oldfashioned to our eyes, but it was the state of the art during the middle years of the 20th century. Wartime always brings death and destruction, but it also sees huge advances in science and technology. When the life of a nation is at stake, no effort is spared to produce new and innovative gizmos that keep us one step ahead of the opposition. With the knowledge gained from the World War II years, printed circuits replaced conventional wiring in much electronic equipment, such as radio and television sets. They became standard in motor cars and aircraft. The size and weight of equipment was reduced. Reliability was improved. Turning out such products had become the job of women whilst the men were away at the front. No longer were they satisfied in returning to the kitchen sink. Women had new knowledge that their husbands did not possess. It was only right that they should build on them by continuing to develop both their freedom and the skills that they had gained. A woman's place was not always to be in the home. Some men did not like it. They had to lump it. The development of far smaller and more compact integrated circuits made printed circuits obsolete in the early 1970s. It did not matter. Women had moved on to greater things. By the end of the 1970s there would be a woman in 10 Downing Street.

Below centre: What a mucky job. But, someone has to do it. Cleaning out the drains is one of those tasks that we are glad that someone else does. Collecting the rubbish from dustbins or being a rat catcher are other jobs for someone else. No matter how you dress them up, these are tasks that are not filled with glamour. The highways' hygiene officer, refuse disposal operative or rodent control agent can keep their titles along with their jobs. The only question that should be asked is why are they so poorly paid? They fulfil an essential role that we would not choose and then fail to reward them. This photograph was taken out of the city centre, perhaps in one of the pretty rural villages of Derbyshire. The clue is the registration plate of the Albion wagon. YRB means that the vehicle was registered in the shire, not in the city, or town as it was when this scene was captured. Cyclists will look at the drain cover with a feeling of annoyance. They seemed to have been designed with one purpose in mind. It must have been a bike hater who first came up with the idea of putting bars and spaces in the covers that pointed down the street. Why else would anyone have come up with a cover in which you could jam your front wheel and disappear over the front handlebars?

Bottom: Remember the old school photographs when we were all taken out onto the field? The whole school was lined up on chairs and PE benches for the annual snap. They are best recalled for the time when Freddie Grimshaw stood at one end. As the camera started to pan across the scene he ducked down, ran round the back and got himself photographed twice in the same shot by appearing again at the other end. He even escaped six of the best because he had left school that summer before the photograph came out! Looking carefully at this posed picture, it does not look as though he got a job with Burrows, Sturgess and Severn, though it would be hard to tell under the peaked caps and uniform coats of the chaps at the end. The workforce of the long established mineral water manufacturers had gathered for this group shot in 1929. The company had been established nearly 80 years before, in 1850. As well as making fizzy pop, Burrows, Sturgess and Severn was also a wine and spirit merchant. There was a plant that also bottled beer, stout and cider. The company occupied several premises. Its administration was handled at the sales offices and stores on Curzon Street. Bottling took place at Abbey Street and the mineral water factory was at the Spa Works in Woods Lane.

Below: The composing room of the Derby Daily Express in the early 1930s relied on the skills of the typesetter to get the column inches correctly aligned and ready for the presses. It was to be another half century before computers began to take over the job that these men proudly did. That change only came after a lot of bitter wrangling, but that is another story. The first daily to appear on local newsstands was the Derby Daily Telegraph. It was only just the first. It came out a mere 20 minutes before its competitor, the Derby Daily Gazette. The paper belonged to Eliza Pike, whose husband had started the Derby Reporter from offices on the Corn Market. When the first edition of the Telegraph was published it cost just a halfpenny. Eliza held the reins until her death in 1905. The Express provided added competition in 1884. In those days there were several editions each day. The rivalry between the Telegraph and the Express continued until 1932, when the two papers merged. The new publication, costing one penny, kept both names in its title for a while. It became the Daily Evening Telegraph in late 1932. The paper moved from Albert Street to Meadow Road in 1979. Here it had access to all the latest technology. The Derby Express was reborn in 1986 as a free newspaper, relying on advertising for its funding. It soon built its circulation, being read in over 130,000 homes.

The manufacture of porcelain in the locality began in 1750. A Huguenot refugee, André Planché, and Staffordshire potter, William Duesbury, opened the Derby China Factory. After a visit by George III in 1773, the town was granted a patent to mark the china with a crown, and the local product was known thereafter as Crown Derby. In 1756 Duesbury established another factory. Advertising itself as 'the second Dresden', it produced finely modelled, palely coloured figures that resembled Chelsea ware and Meissen wares. Flowers and colourful insects were favourite decorations of the serviceware. Duesbury purchased the Chelsea works in 1770. He began a trend towards a neoclassical style. During the last decades of the century the painting of the wares achieved a marked excellence. The unglazed figures, some based on those produced at Sèvres in France, became the most delicate and expensive that were manufactured. This photograph was taken in the building that was the old Union Workhouse. Built to a design by local man John Mason in 1839, it was depressingly known as the Bastille. Derby Crown Porcelain Company opened in Osmaston Road in 1875 and the works pictured began operation in 1877-78. After a visit from Queen Victoria in 1890, the company was allowed to use 'Royal' in its title. Royal Crown Derby was born. It became part of the Allied Potteries Group in 1964. When Derby became a city in 1977 the new council received gifts to be added to the city regalia. Included in these was a piece of the finest Royal Derby chinaware.

Left: These brave firefighters were part of the Derby Auxiliary Fire Service (AFS), based at Walker Lane in 1940. The AFS was just one branch of the Civil Defence that grew up in the late 1930s as the country prepared for war. When the balloon went up many of these organisations were activated and stood ready for duty. Volunteers trained at Allestree Hall. Special training that helped them work on high ladders was carried out at the old Assembly Rooms. Members were expected to be busy during the war. The lessons learned from observing the bombing raids in Spain during its recent civil war were taken seriously. The AFS was ready to swing into action at the drop of a hat or the clang of a fire bell. Walker Lane had an old Dennis fire appliance. Its 80 foot turntable and ladder was not the easiest piece of equipment to handle. The ladder swayed in the wind. The crew had to hang on tight to it as a colleague went up to the top. It took a strong nerve. These brave souls had plenty of that. They went out when bombs were falling around them. Despite that, they served the citizens of Derby with a coolness and professionalism that was a credit to their dedication. They might have been nervous on the inside, but it never stopped them from doing their duty. The AFS became the National Fire Service in 1941. The Walker Lane crew included a woman. Gender differences were not important when there was a job to be done and a war to be won.

Below: Derby was quick to see the problems that the motor car was likely to bring to its streets. Through traffic was light by today's proportions. But, it was heavy enough in the 1920s to encourage the highways department to make plans to take it round the town. It would be another 40 years before the inner ring road was completed in an attempt to keep town centre traffic on the move. Manor Road, the outer ring road, was opened in June 1929. As part of an advertising venture, a fleet of vans and lorries belonging to Burrows, Sturgess and Severn were on show, stretching several hundred yards down the road. The drivers for this company of bottlers, wine and spirit merchants and soft drinks manufacturers stood to attention outside the cabs of their vehicles. The directors and company officials made sure that they took centre stage. We can work out the rank of those on the empty carriageway. Each person's importance was reflected in his style of headgear. Bowler hats for the top brass, trilbies and homburgs for middle management and a flat cap for the lesser mortal. One of the products of which the company was especially proud was its 'Iron Brew'. This was not to be confused with that concoction of AG Barr, 'Irn Bru', very popular north of the border. In 1935 the Derby firm opened premises on Ashbourne Road, in between the Methodist Church and the Council School. The church has since been demolished and the school became Ashgate School. Burrows, Sturgess and Severn is now just a faint memory.

To a politician the name Hoover means the American president who was around during the bootleg and gangster years of 1929-33. A policeman might immediately be reminded of J Edgar Hover who was the boss man of the FBI for nearly 50 years. To anyone else it means a vacuum cleaner. To millions of housewives it also meant some release from the lengthy toil that was housework. The Hoover company moved from making some of the world's first vacuum cleaners into manufacturing many other electrical labour saving devices. This grateful woman was demonstrating one of their first washing machines. In the late 1930s the washtub with the hand cranked mangle was a boon. She had grown up used to lifting sodden clothes from the old tub with a pair of wooden tongs. Having wrung them out, they were steered through a heavy

mangle before getting their final airing on the line. The American Alva Fisher made the first electric washing machine in 1907. It was given the mighty name of 'Thor'. There was little significant development in washing machines from the period when this picture was taken until about 1960. Designers faced two problems. The motor had to be powerful to deal with a 50 lb sink full equivalent of wet washing, particularly when the water was to be extracted by spinning. Then, several kilowatts of power, equal to every bar and then some on an electric fire being turned on, were needed to heat up the water for one load. It was the arrival of twin tubs and then automatics that advanced the lot of the housewife once more. Vincent Bendix, another American, invented the first automatic that washed, rinsed and dried without too much interference from its owner.

Below: From the registration plate on this milk float, the scene probably dates from about 1970. The shiny electric cart was a far cry from Smith's horse and cart that used to clatter along the streets bringing us our daily delivery. After World War II the government was concerned about the state of the nation's health. Rationing had meant that our diets were not as rich in vitamins as they should have been. The birth of the welfare state made children's nourishment a priority. Schools had to provide a hot meal at lunchtime. Free milk, in little one third of a pint bottles, were issued at break time to all primary schoolchildren. The teachers were canny enough to get the milk monitor to collect the drinking straws. The straw monitor would wash them before being given out by the art monitor in craft or paint blowing lessons. That continued until Margaret Thatcher, Minister for Education, took free milk off the agenda in the early 1970s. Many education authorities brought back milk for youngsters in our schools in later years, but charged for it. During the 60s and 70s advertising slogans such as 'Drinka pinta milka day' continued to encourage us to

keep up the healthy habit. Northern Dairies was one of the three main dairies that brought us our deliveries. The others were the Co-op and Hadfield's. In 1971, the comedian, Benny Hill, was to have a number one hit record with 'Ernie, the fastest milkman in the west'. Those of us who remember the song cannot look a milkman in the eye without thinking of his gold tops rattling in the crate!

Bottom: The poster on the side of Webb's tripe van, with the smashed up front, says 'And Sudden Death'. Hopefully, this was not a prophecy come true. It is more likely to have been a mock up as a publicity stunt advertising the film showing at the nearby Coliseum picture house on London Road. The driver of the breakdown truck does not seem too bothered about the situation. He is just passing the Alexandra Rooms. They were the purpose built studios of WW Winters, the well known local photographer. The premises had been built by Henry Isaac Stevens. He was a famous church builder of his day. The shape of the windows in the Alexandra Rooms owes much to Stevens' church links. They were named after the wife of Edward VII. She was Alexandra Caroline Mary Charlotte Louisa Julia, Princess of Schleswig-Holstein-Sonderburg-Glocksburg, Princess of Wales. Fortunately for sign writers everywhere she became Queen Alexandra. Mr Winters, the studio owner, had a long connection with Edward VII. He was his official photographer on royal visits to the Midlands. However, Winters was very much his own man and a God fearing one as well. On one trip to Chatsworth, the King asked Winters to accompany him for a photo shoot. As it was a Sunday Mr Winters told His Highness he would have to wait until Monday. The King did as he was told! Winters later became a priest.

Below: The engine house of the Derby Playhouse contained all the sound mixing equipment and projection aids that were needed in the 1960s and 1970s. The Playhouse had developed from the Little Repertory Theatre on Becket Street that was to become Wilkins Memorial Hall. It opened in 1948, after the Grand Theatre had closed. The Little Theatre was really just a private club, started by a group of frustrated Thespians and theatre buffs. In those early postwar years there was still a desire for live entertainment and the theatre flourished. By 1952 it had moved to Sacheverel Street, occupying a building that had once been home to a Baptist Sunday School. It reopened as the Derby Playhouse. Among its company of actors was James Beck. He went on to great success as a member of the cast of 'Dad's Army', the long running BBC TV comedy series. He played the part of the wide boy and black marketeer. Despite being badly damaged by fire in 1956, it was back presenting plays the following year. When this photograph was taken, the Playhouse had begun screening films during the summer, in rotation with presenting plays. The engineer had a lot to do, flicking his switches and twiddling his dials all at the right time. No wonder he had a big box of Kleenex above his head to mop his brow. This Playhouse closed in 1975 and became the Ajanta, showing Asian films. That closed in 1978 and the building was knocked down in 1989. A new 500 seater Playhouse opened in the Eagle Centre in 1975.

Right: This company is now part of Reckitt Toiletry Products. It began life as FW Hampshire in the old Derby silk mill. The picture is of workers in the Sinfin Lane factory where it really became established. The young women were carefully inspecting and packing little tins of Snowfire Cream. It was a best seller for the company. The moisturising cream could restore dry skin to a gentle smoothness and get rid of those awful wrinkles and crows' feet. At least that was what we were told. The packets were sold to chemists for displaying on the their counters near the till. The idea was to tempt a woman into buying a tin of cream just as she was collecting her prescription or paying for a can of Andrews' Liver Salts. Modern super-markets try to pull the same trick by siting little packets of sweets near the checkout. The small aluminium containers of the magic cream retailed for 3d (1p). The grander opal jars set you back a princely 1s 6d (7.5p). The workforce at FW Hampshire's factory was mainly a female environment. The work was not well paid and could be very repetitive. Quality control was important. Production had to be carried out in hygienic surroundings. It would not have been good for business to turn out a contaminated product that a woman was going to spread on her skin. The girls at the workbench wore clean overalls and caps just to make sure.

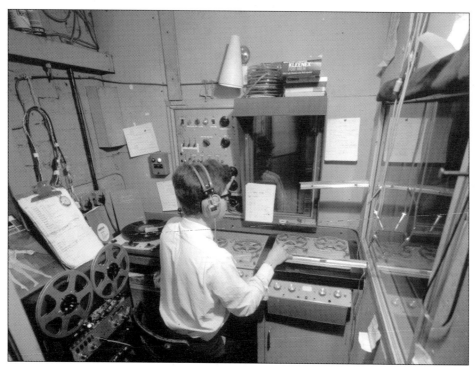

Changing techniques, constant standards

It was the death of his first wife, Isabella that led Joseph Mason to take up his brother's offer of help and to relinquish landscape gardening to turn his attentions to varnish making; Joseph had received some education at a time when the majority could neither read nor write he had a beautiful, strong copperplate style of handwriting. Isabella's premature death had left Joseph with four young sons to care for and he apprenticed them all in his new trade. This stood them in good stead when after the end of the Napoleonic Wars in 1814 they had a sound economic base at a time of great hardship in Derby, a time characterised by food shortages and high unemployment. The business operated from the three-storey building in Derwent Street, and their varnishes were mixed on site by painters and thinned to produce either a matt or glossy paint-like substance.

From the very beginning, in 1800, the name Mason was synonymous with high quality paint finishes among coach builders. At that time paint production was a very different process from that of today, early company documents specify four coats of lead, seven coats of 'rough stuff', one coat of lead putty and face, one coat of lead then smooth with sandpaper, a further coat of lead, sandpaper again, three coats of colour, a coat of glazing, four coats of varnish and a coat of best wearing 'body'; between each coat the surface was rubbed well.

Joseph remarried in 1810 and two of his sons married the daughters of Ann, his second wife. However his health deteriorated and he died in 1826, leaving the company to his widow along with shares in the Derby canal as well as sundry government securities. The eldest son, William (born 1788) and the youngest, Joseph (born 1793) both continued running the company after their father's death, the other two started their own business in the same field, Robert (born 1789) set up as a Japanner, oil and colour merchant at 30 Exeter Street and Ford Lane as Robert Mason & Co., John (born 1791) traded at 52 Ashborne Road as a varnish maker, colour merchant, grainer and tool maker.

Above: *Early can labels.*
Below: *Workmen at the varnish factory circa 1890.*

The company's products were in high demand both at home and abroad, a number of cans and barrels bearing the name Joseph Mason & Co have recently been discovered in the company retail stores section of the Lower Garry Fort (now a museum) in Canada - Mason's was obviously a trusted name in the mid 1800s in this settlement.

Joseph Mason & Co moved to Burton Road, Derby in 1831 and in 1869, a chimney known as Mason's Folly made its appearance on the site; it was designed in Moorish style and became a great talking point for the population of Derby. The idea of having such a large chimney was to take the noxious fumes high into the atmosphere and well away from the town; this was a very commendable motive but unfortunately failed to take into account the prevailing winds which despite all the carefully laid plans carried the fumes directly onto the surrounding houses. However it was acclaim which was the order of the day as far as the standard of the products was concerned when the company achieved international recognition in 1867 by being awarded a prize medal for 'Excellence of Varnishes and Colours' at the Paris Universal Exhibition.

The business was put up for sale in 1871 and was purchased by Henry Edward Ayre who was advised to find himself a reliable source of income by his prospective father-in-law. As Mr Sissons of Hull was himself a varnish manufacturer it is not surprising that he suggested the purchase of Joseph Mason & Co., thus enlarging the family empire.

The centenary of the founding of the company was marked in 1900 with the acquisition of the present seven-and-a-half acre site on Nottingham Road. A purpose-built factory was built in 1902 under the supervision of a member of the Ayre family.

King George V and Queen Mary visited the Joseph Mason stand at the 1933 Royal Agricultural Show in Derby, where they viewed the highly detailed scale model of the Irish State Coach which had been painted with Joseph Mason's paints.

Above centre: *Mason's Folly Burton Road.*
Top: *The visit of King George V and Queen Mary to the Joseph Mason stand at the Derby Royal Agricultural Show in 1933.*

Joseph Mason & Co's progressive approach put them amongst the first manufacturers of high-grade cellulose finishes and after they had recognised the potential of alkyd resin-based synthetics in 1936, they became one of the first paint producers in the UK to manufacture their own resin. War-time ambulances built by Rolls-Royce were painted in Masopar Coach enamel, produced by Mason's.

In 1954, a company lorry displaying part of the range of products manufactured at the company took part in the Celebration Parade commemorating 750 years since the granting of the Charter to the Town of Derby by King John.

The 1960s saw the introduction of large and sophisticated commercial vehicles and Joseph Mason once again led the field becoming, in 1968, the first UK paint manufacturer to produce QDP (quick drying polyurethane - a one-pack enamel for transport vehicles). This contributed considerably to the emergence of Joseph Mason as the market leader for commercial vehicle refinishing paints. Their 'Intense Black Cellulose Enamel' was supplied to Rolls Royce Ltd. at this time.

High standards of product quality and customer service are widely acknowledged and demonstrated by the granting of the Royal Warrant of Appointment as tradesmen to HM the Queen as Manufacturers of Coach Paints in 1982, making them one of a privileged group of only 800 companies in the country. The important recognition of accreditation to BS5750 Part 1 and ISO9001 followed in 1987.

Mason's advanced technology and expertise were in demand in 1982 when the Venice-Simplon Orient Express, the train immortalised by Agatha Christie, once again began its twice-weekly luxury train service between London, Paris, Milan and Venice. The rolling stock needed to be as authentic as craftsmanship and scholarship could make it, and the wagon-lits and British pullmans were equipped, to the last brass fitting, to the very pattern of the original decor. Four meticulously decorated first-class carriages provided accommodation on the first leg of the journey from London to Folkestone. Each of the beautifully and individually adorned carriages was meticulously decorated in Mason's

Above: An advertisement for Masolac Intense Black Cellulose enamel from the 1950s. *Below:* A group of Mason employees on a visit to London to celebrate the company's 150th anniversary in 1950.

In common with many other branches of industry, vehicle painting has been the subject of continuous process of change in both methods and materials. This has taken place gradually, almost imperceptibly and it is often only when old coachpainters begin to reminisce about the days of their youth or when you read books printed about hundred years ago that the very profound changes become evident. Many changes have arisen from the progress that has been made in paint manufacture. The modern painter expects simply to remove a lid from a paint tin and start his work, he has probably never heard of 'slab and muller' which was so important in the paintshops of the past, nor does he need to concern himself with pigmentations, or the material he is painting - nowadays all these matters have been addressed by the paint chemist beforehand. Many of the problems that faced coachpainters of the past have been eliminated by the changes that have taken place in vehicle construction. Most work is now carried out on metal and plastics. By contrast in the early days, most work involved wooden panels and leather stretched and glued to a wood base. All this involved a great deal of filling and rubbing which accounted for the majority of the time spent, and therefore the cost, of the job. Many of the old skills have been lost but have been replaced by a very high standard of technology which

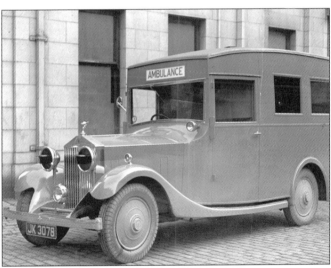

materials and the carriage names and signs worked in Mason's writers colour and gold leaf; parts of the interior were coated with Mason's varnish.

In 1998, Joseph Mason, now trading as Mason Coatings PLC acquired a graphics division with the very latest digital printing system. This makes them the only company in the UK able to provide both the paint and the decals (the vinyl lettering and pictures) for commercial vehicles. Mason products are used on vehicles used by such household names as BP, Marks & Spencer, TNT and numerous bus companies operating across the country (they have the capacity to handle complete livery changes for large fleets of vehicles). However Mason paints are not found exclusively on the lorries which speed up and down the motorway network, but also on agricultural machinery, railway and waterway stock. Also manufacturers of high performance coatings, Mason's supplies anti-corrosion and hygiene coating systems for bridges, pipelines and hospitals, as well as industrial coatings for gas cylinders and steel drums.

Above left: *A wartime ambulance painted in Masopar Coach Enamel.* ***Top:*** *A company van used in 1948.* ***Below:*** *A company lorry with some of its products, on its way to a parade in 1954.*

could not fail to impress the old-time coachpainters were it possible to show them round a modern paintshop.

Modern paints consist of four main ingredients - resin, which holds the paint together and sticks to the painted surface this is also known as binder and medium varnish, pigment, to provide colour and anti-corrosive properties (among other things), solvent to dissolve the resin and adjust the viscosity to allow for easy application and additives eg driers, anti-skinning agents which improve the properties of the material. The most important of these ingredients is the resin, as this dictates the final type of paint, the area of use and the basic properties of the paint such as durability, drying time and overcoating time. Mason Coatings is almost unique in the paint industry in that for a large part of their 200 year history they have manufactured the bulk of their own resins. This facility has enabled the company to formulate new resins to meet market requirements and give them a competitive edge.

In the early days all resin manufacture would be carried out using naturally occurring materials imported from all around the world, eg Dammar resin, a

gum which exudes from trees found in Malaya, Shellac, a brittle resin mainly from India based on the bodies of dead Lac beetles and Linseed Oil, a sticky liquid obtained from the Flax plant. The raw materials would be assembled by the 'varnish master' and processed in a small open container containing probably about 20 gallons, over an open fire to a secret recipe known only to the varnish master and passed on from father to son. The process control would be very rudimentary and would depend entirely on the skill of the individual. Viscosity would be checked by the speed of flow of the mixture from the stirring stick, temperature would be judged by the sound given out when the varnish maker spat into the hot liquid. Each varnish

Above: *The Orient Express, the British rake of which was restored using paint and varnish.*
Right: *A coach from the Royal Mews.*

master would add his own secret ingredient, such as a spider's web which he would claim gave additional beneficial properties to the end product. The basic process has remained unchanged for 200 years, with raw materials being assembled and heated together until the chemical reaction is complete. However the nature of the raw materials, the manufacturing equipment required, the essential chemistry and the personnel requirements have changed dramatically over that time. The majority of raw materials used in modern resin technology are now man-made and are products of today's oil or chemical industry. A modern resin plant is a very expensive, enclosed, high quality steel reactor vessel with automated raw material feed, inbuilt stirring, vacuum distillation and heating/cooling capable of producing up to 10,000 litres of resin per batch.

Above centre: *An aerial view of the premises in the 1950s...* **Below:** *...and today.*

With such a history of expertise and innovation, Mason's is well-placed to meet ongoing and new demands placed upon it. A good example of this is its response to the Environmental Protection Act, 1990 which laid down guidelines for local authorities to implement aimed at preventing or reducing the release of certain substances, particularly solvents, into the environment; Masons responded by investing further in research and development, producing a number of water-based 'Compliant Coatings', which are highly regarded in the industry today.

The Mason business philosophy is one of continual improvement and a commitment to long-term development and research. This means that Masons are always at the forefront of new technologies and innovative paint and decal systems. Though employing very different materials and techniques, Mason Coatings continues to offer products of the same high quality as its founder over 200 years ago.

Marketing the past

Markets have played a central part of Derby's economy for centuries. In that time Derby's markets have witnessed bull baiting, ox roasts, pillories and stocks as well as the sale of millions of head of cattle. Today the thriving cattle market is one of the top six in the country. And the wholesale fruit and vegetable market is one the nation's top twenty venues.

Traditional shopping is not forgotten either with thriving retail markets: the Market Hall and Eagle Centre offering city centre shoppers a choice and diversity of goods to suit all needs. Elsewhere the district market at Allenton serves the needs of the south eastern part of the city.

Nor is that the end of the matter: with increasingly popular car boot sales at the cattle market on Sunday mornings and fortnightly Saturday auction sales being held there too Derby's historic reputation as a major market centre is being upheld right into the 21st century.

Derby has been a market town for a thousand years. In 1204 however King John bestowed upon the town a charter which formally authorised

Right: The Market Hall in the 1950s. **Below:** *The cattle market around 1955.*

markets to be held twice weekly. Unfortunately for those with goods to sell the charter also allowed the town burgesses to impose tolls on market traders.

In fact the earliest known market charter had been given to Derby by Henry II in 1155 though even that document refers to an even earlier charter granted by Henry I.

King John's charter stated that the men of Derbyshire and Nottinghamshire were to come to Derby Market on Thursdays and Fridays 'with their carts and sumpter beasts'. It is interesting to note that Friday would remain the main market day in Derby for the next eight hundred years.

known. Between these and what is now the western edge of Market Place ran the narrow thoroughfare known as Rotten Row. The Market Place was further encumbered by the Market Cross and the Old Town Hall, a dilapidated brick building of two storeys. The upper storey, reached by a flight of stairs outside the building, was used as the council chamber and the ground floor as the borough gaol.

In the middle of the 19th century Friday was still the principal market day for all goods and provisions but markets were also held on Wednesday for butter and vegetables and on Saturdays for meat and vegetables. The market for cattle, sheep and pigs was held in the Morledge on Tuesdays.

Despite the additional accommodation eventually provided to the inhabitants of the borough, and its surrounding neighbourhood by the extension of the

Derby markets grew and prospered with the growth of the town. Not even the Great Plague of 1665 slowed business too much - a temporary market was established at Nun's Green where stalls were simply placed further apart and money dipped in vinegar before payment - whilst market traders chewed tobacco in the belief that this would act as a preventative against the dread disease.

Derby's Market Place in the 18th century was very small, the western side being encumbered by a range of buildings known as the Piazzas behind which were the shambles, as abattoirs were then

Above left: *Some of the fruit and vegetable merchants in the Wholesale Market, 1950s.*
Top: *Sheep at the market in the mid 1950s.*

markets and the shambles, there was still a good deal of overcrowding: shortage of space made transacting business often extremely inconvenient. A new shambles was occupied chiefly by butchers from country villages; it was however a Mr Wild, a gardener who lived in Osmaston Road, who was the first to open a shop at the top of the Piazza or Market Head and his example was soon followed by others.

As the population and size of the borough continued to grow it became increasingly obvious that the Market Place was too small. Eventually the corporation purchased premises and built a new market on the south side of the old market but communicating with it. That new market place was on the same site as the present Market Hall and consisted of a hundred shops for butchers, a butter market and a covered space for selling fruit and vegetables.

The Market Hall
In 1866 Derby was buzzing with the excitement of the opening of the country's first purpose built undercover market which had been built at the cost of £29,000.

This was a shopping revolution; an event in relative terms comparable to the opening of the first huge out of town shopping malls which have sprung up across Britain in recent years.

The new Market Hall was crammed as the Secretary of State for War, the Duke of Devonshire, performed the opening ceremony to the accompaniment of 600 choristers singing the Messiah. The hall accommodated almost 40 butcher's shops and 150 stalls, 40 of them being situated round the balcony.

Above: *An aerial view of Derby with the Bus Station in the left foreground and Morledge Open Market just behind.*

During the intervening years there have been many changes to the building, mostly of a superficial nature, as successive councils tried to ensure that the Market Hall kept abreast of the times.

A major refurbishment however took place in 1938 which saw the Victorian interior change to a then contemporary 1930s style. The ornate ironwork on the balcony was clad with oak-veneered panels and the balcony withdrawn from use. That austere image continued until 1986 when it was discovered that the building's supports had moved over time. To preserve this local landmark, a grade two listed building, the council now organised a second and major refurbishment.

Renovation began with the removal of the old floor. To the architect's surprise workers discovered one of Derby's medieval streets and two sixty foot deep wells. One well was found directly under Camps butchers shop. The work took two years to complete and the austerity of the 1930s look gave way to the original Victorian grandeur: the ornate ironwork can be admired once again following the reopening presided over by HRH Princess Margaret in 1989.

Adjoining the main building are the poultry and fish markets. The Fish Market in Lock Up Yard is on the site of an old gaol house. A glance upwards on the wall above the fish stalls reveals the marks where the cells used to join the main building.

The Eagle Centre Market
This imposing modern building built in 1975 is a classic example of modern architecture and stands on the site of the ancient Cockpitt Hill street market; here in years gone by barrowboys traded their wares.

The Eagle Centre market was built opposite the old open-air Morledge market which not too long ago stood on the site of today's Crown Court. The Eagle Centre was built to replace the Morledge market which had in fact only been built in 1933.

In the early years there were problems with the building's structure and layout so in 1992 the council decided to refurbish and redesign the interior. The results are excellent and the market is heated in winter and cooled in summer.

The result is a first class modern shopping facility for both residents and visitors to the city. It is far removed from the windswept market of old where the cry of famous traders like 'Mad Harry' echoed around Cockpitt Hill.

The Wholesale Market
Derby's market revolution in the 1960s meant a short move away from the town centre for the Wholesale Market. Chequers Road on the north eastern side of the city was selected as the new site because of its easy access to and from the A52. The new Wholesale Market opened in conjunction with the new Cattle Market on 5 June 1970 replacing the old market which soon gave way to the inner ring road. The new Wholesale Market was designed by Miss P Woods of the Borough Architects department and built by W Walkerdine Ltd.

The 'old' Wholesale Market had in fact only moved across the river from the Market Place in 1925 when suitable land with premises had been purchased from the government for £27,000. Alterations and additions including the provision of warehouses and banana rooms brought the capital expenditure to £32,000 but some property and plant were sold bringing the net capital cost to £29,847.

In 1925 there was some opposition to the suitability of that first 'new' Wholesale Market but after the first few years of trading it was generally agreed that it had turned out to be an excellent venture. The only disadvantage being that it was not very accessible being surrounded by narrow streets and bounded by the canal. To improve the position some ground, previously used as allotments, was purchased to provide an entrance from Meadow Road.

Above: Brochures promoting the markets.

Barrowboys

Street trading from handcarts goes back centuries and was a feature of Derby's streets until the town centre was revamped in the 1960s. It has been allowed to re-emerge in recent years, though on a strictly controlled scale.

Street traders are obliged to obtain a licence from the Markets Department of the council and are allocated a pitch on the Promenade or in either Albion or East Street, close to what was once Cockpitt Hill, where the barrowboys once thronged selling all manner of goods. 'The Hill' was once a hive of activity and is now sadly missed as a feature of City life.

Allenton Market

Derby's growth during the 1950s led to the Council's decision to build a satellite market in the suburbs. And so in 1962 Allenton Market came into being.

The general layout is the same as the old Morledge Market in the city but has the added benefit of being completely covered. Throughout its relatively short history Allenton Market has proved to be another feather in Derby's marketing cap having been well patronised since its opening and attracting additional custom to its weekly flea and craft market.

The Cattle Market

Anyone looking to buy a cow at Derby's Cattle Market on a Sunday morning will at first be disappointed to discover that instead of cattle they are offered almost anything else other than four footed beasts. On the other hand they may well be tempted by those myriad of other goods on offer. The Cattle Market is home every Sunday to a thriving car boot sale where up to 600 'car booters' offer a vast range of items for sale.

The Cattle Market was moved to its present site in Chequers Road in the late 1960s and officially opened by Lord Hives in June 1970. The area was previously known as The Meadows, a fact commemorated by the name of the Meadows Inn at the market. The 'new' market has altered very little since it was built - which is to the credit of its architects. It still caters well considering the substantial increase in trade since it was finished. The market is classed as amongst the top ten cattle markets in the country for its quality of livestock.

Derby's Cattle Market too was designed by the Borough Architects Department, the project leader

*Above: A recent brochure promoting Derby's markets. **Top**: The fish market in the 1950s.*

being R W Walker; the design with three sales rings as one of its architectural features was designed for a throughput of 100,000 head of cattle annually.

Before the second world war Derby's old Cattle Market had in fact sold 150,000 head each year. The old Cattle Market had been on the site now made unrecognisable by the ring road and car park since 1861 and had four auction sale rings. Most of the building on that old site had however only been carried out in 1897 when £15,000 was spent turning the site into a then modern market including a new pig market and the conversion of stables into a market office. The 23 acres of land for building the present Cattle Market, abattoir and the wholesale market, at the Meadows off Nottingham Road was purchased in 1955.

Care of livestock is very important and the drovers, auctioneers and Animal Welfare Officers are all well trained in the treatment of animals.

Market days are vibrant affairs with the constant movement of bawling squealing cattle interspersed with the monotonous drone of the auctioneer's voice and the crack of his hammer to conclude the sale. Our forefathers would have witnessed exactly the same sights and sounds - only the venue has changed.

Monthly horse sales and the annual Fatstock Show make up a comprehensive calendar of events which attract visitors from all over the country.

And it is not only cattle which are auctioned at the cattle market; local auctioneers hold fortnightly Saturday auctions there with viewing taking place on the preceding day.

Although all types of goods change hands in Derby's many markets perhaps the only thing a man cannot buy is a wife. Once however Thomas Bott a local ne'er-do-well sold his wife in the Market Place for 18 pence to a man from Langley Common. With a halter round her waist Bott then handed his wife over to her new 'owner'. How times change!

Top and above left: *The French Market pictured in 1999.* ***Below:*** *Inside the recently refurbished Market Hall.*

Tomlinson - the complete solution

The Tomlinson Group plc, based in Derby's City Road, is today a leading force within the Midlands construction and civil engineering industries. The group made up of GF Tomlinson Building Ltd, GF Tomlinson & Sons Ltd, GF Tomlinson Construction Ltd and the Total Hire & Sales Ltd business provides services that cover the full spectrum of construction. The group's enviable reputation in the building, civil engineering and utility sectors has been built up over more than a century of repeat business and now covers an operational area from Yorkshire to the Home Counties and from mid-Wales to the east coast.

George Frank Tomlinson the founder of today's huge business was born in 1866, the son of George Tomlinson a well known Derby estate agent and surveyor.

On leaving school at the age of seventeen G F Tomlinson joined his uncle Joseph Tomlinson, a

Above: The firm's founder, George Frank Tomlinson.
Right, both pictures: The founder's sons Cyril and George. Below: Building a bridge on the A6 in 1906.

road builder, and a colourful figure in Derby. Young George acted as a timekeeper and gradually gained more responsibility.

In 1892, aged 26, George decided to set up a business of his own as a civil engineering contractor.

Four years after founding the firm George Tomlinson bought the business' current premises in City Road, Derby, a site ideally situated on the river bank where there was a commercial wharf, as well as one which provided easy access to St Mary's Goods Yard, then an important railhead.

An early contract was to construct a brick culvert from the Coach & Horses public house on Alfreton Road to the Nottingham Road/Stores Road junction. This was soon followed by the construction of the Eggington Sewage Disposal works.

The foundation for the new Cupolas at Park Gate Foundry at Rotherham was another contract about that time when there were few experienced contracting firms around. Within a few years a large drainage contract was being undertaken as far away as Romford in Essex, a project on which 300 men were employed.

There was little mechanisation then and most of the work was undertaken by hand, hence the large number of men involved. Goods were delivered by rail to the nearest station and hauled to the site by horse and cart or by steam engine. The demand for more up to date transport saw the firm purchase one of the early Foden steam lorries.

In 1906 bridge building was developing and the brick built bridge adjacent to the old railway crossing at Swadlincote was constructed by the firm as well as the bridge over the River Derwent in Matlock town. A few years later the Coalville bridge complex was also built by George Tomlinson.

Housing developments were very much part of the firm's work in the form of main drainage and road construction. Many of the streets in Burton on Trent were developed in this period. At the start of the first world war in 1914 the firm was carrying out work on a very large development in the Osmaston Park Road area of Derby.

After the first world war George Tomlinson's two sons George and Cyril joined their father providing the impetus for more growth and diversification.

During the inter-war years several new bridges were built and older ones widened. One was the bridge at Rowsley over the River Derwent, others included bridges at Hathersage Calver.

So great was the demand for contractors just after the Great War that some councils were almost pleading for experienced contractors to undertake work. At this time the firm undertook a large drainage contract with an outfall into the sea at Aberystwyth. And in 1923 the firm had the unusual contract to resurface St Peter's Street in Derby with wood block paving - the contract specified that the firm had just six weeks to complete the job.

Above: *Labourers pictured in the early 1900s.*
Top: *Building the foundations for Derby Corporation House in 1937.*

Diversification continued to be the order of the day and Tomlinsons was responsible for laying the track and erecting all the tram poles in Derby. The firm also gained the contract for track laying and overhead installation in Burton. Gas main laying was also being widely carried out by the firm both in and around Derby, as was the laying of electric cables.

A Matlock and Matlock Bath drainage scheme which involved land which was almost entirely in solid rock was undertaken in 1923: one can only imagine the difficulty this posed without today's modern equipment.

In 1924 the firm constructed the new Eggington Bridge on the A38 Derby-Burton Road in order to by-pass the old Monks Bridge over the River Dove. At the time the bridge created great interest as it was the longest single span bridge ever constructed in reinforced concrete - 139 feet: on completion the bridge was loaded with several steam rollers, steam lorries hauling heavy loads to test for any defects! That bridge now forms the South bound carriageway of the A38 its twin having been built in the late 1960s.

The limited company of G F Tomlinson & Sons Ltd was formed in 1926. A large contract around that time was the construction of the sluice gates across the River Derwent at Spondon in order to

provide cooling water for British Celanese. This also involved laying an 18 inch diameter pipe under the river bed for the supply of water; divers had to be used for the project. At the same time the company extended the Celanese factory with all necessary roads and drainage works.

Tomlinsons were also responsible in this period for laying out the sites for the International Combustion

Top: *The third Caterpillar tractor imported from the USA for the construction of Allestree Golf Course, 1930.* **Above right:** *Radio Derby.* **Right:** *Pride Park, Derby County FC's ground.*

Following the great stock market crash of 1929 the world went into recession and many firms failed to survive. During the economic slump in 1930 however Tomlinsons was engaged on straightening and improving the River Derwent just south of the town.

In 1931 the firm was awarded a contract to build the Hoo Ash Reservoir and to lay 31 miles of water distribution pipes through north Leicestershire; at the same time it was also extending the Derwent Valley Aqueduct from King Corner Chaddesden to Sawley.

Allestree Village came on to main drainage in 1933 and a new disposal works was also built there. At the same time Little Eaton Water works and filter beds were also constructed by Tomlinsons.

In 1936 the firm was responsible for the construction of the platforms and loading docks and for paving the St Mary's Goods Yard in Derby near to the firm's City Road headquarters.

In those inter-war years leisure activities were beginning to come to the fore and a new golf course at Humbledown Farm, now swallowed up by the Mackworth Estate was built in 1936. That was soon followed by the Allestree golf course.

Works and the Pirelli Works at Burton on Trent. Railways were very much to the forefront in those days when large factories were being laid out, these invariably had their own sidings and at that time Tomlinsons had gangs of men who specialised in undertaking such work.

The old Ford Lane bridge at Allestree consisted of railway sleepers tied to wire ropes and in 1926 Tomlinsons built the reinforced concrete bridge which is there today. At the same time the firm also built the bridge over the canal between Chellaston and Swakestone.

In 1929 the firm had a contract tunnelling into the hillside at Sydnope to tap an underground water supply and to lay mains to this village and to Two Dales.

The Coxbench by-pass on the A6 Alfreton Road began at the close of the 1920s and Tomlinsons worked on this from Jack-D-Derby bridge to the Horsley cross roads.

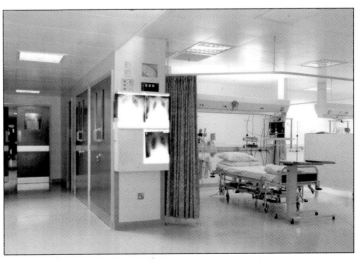

Top: *The Gala Pool in the Queen's Leisure Centre.* **Top right:** *Derby Dance Centre.* **Right:** *Completed refurbishment and upgrade of Derby Royal Infirmary.*

To construct the latter the firm purchased a very modern piece of equipment to eliminate the horse and dobbin cart for earth moving: a two ton Caterpillar tractor - only the second one to be imported into the UK from America. Today one connects that name with the huge monsters that build our motorways, in 1936 the 'monsters' were a little smaller.

Gas supplies to the outlying districts around Derby brought an era of great activity to Tomlinsons as miles of mains were laid each year; similarly electricity cable laying was also spreading and keeping the firm busy.

During the war years of 1939-45 the company was engaged in the building of military installations and on the conversion of factories to undertake war work. The company also constructed many large static water tanks in and about Derby for use in fire fighting should there be a blitz on the town by German bombers.

After the second world war the company reverted to undertaking road works and main drainage for new housing developments for local councils. Work was also undertaken converting factories back from war work to peacetime usage. At the end of the 1950s the company also undertook the reconstruction of the railway bridge at Draycott .

In 1960 Tomlinsons was awarded the contract for the first and the largest stage of the road and main drainage construction on the Mackworth Estate in Derby. This was undertaken using several gangs of men; at the same time a new reservoir was constructed at Hazelwood by the firm.

Top left: *Barry Sewards, Chairman.*
Top right: *The revamped Nottingham Railway Station.* **Above centre:** *The recently restored St Mary's Chapel in Clumber Park.* **Right:***Roy Collis, Construction Director.*

During the latter part of the 1960s there was a great demand for housing both from local authorities and private developers. In that same period there was also a great demand for electricity cable laying which was part of a national scheme to standardise and strengthen the electricity distribution system to meet the demand for a 240 volts supply over the whole country. Among some of the older employees there were a few who had previous experience of this type of work before the war and they were brought together to teach new and younger men their skills.

Within a very short time there were six highly skilled gangs of men undertaking this cable laying work within the Derby and Burton areas and in and around Mansfield.

A cable laying gang would usually consist of about 12 men whose daily task was to excavate 250 yards each day to lay a whole drum of cable. And they cleared up each night before they finished. This type of work lasted for five years until it was suddenly realised that the strengthening of supplies was adequately covered and the whole of Tomlinson's cable-laying organisation was disbanded within a few weeks.

The company strength lay in being able to diversify to meet such set backs and challenges. During the early 1970s the company undertook several small extensions of industrial buildings to the factory complex at Pirelli in Burton on Trent. The largest of these was the new despatch building which can be seen from the main road.

The company has always been experienced in main drainage works and large contracts were carried out in the Stanley and West Hallam area and then the Ockbrook and Borrowash amongst many other smaller ones. Sewage Disposal works, consisting of heavy reinforced underground concrete tanks together with filter bed and their reinforced concrete works, were constructed some from new, some enlarged and modernised, but due to the cut back in public expenditure the demand for this type of work fell from about 1977 onwards.

In 1968 City Plant Hire (Derby) Ltd had been formed with the view of expanding the firm and making use of the plant held by Tomlinsons but not in use.

In 1976 the operations of the plant hire business were moved from City Road to the company's store yard in Alfreton Road where there was plenty of room for development and a new workshop and office complex was built there.

The hire business grew rapidly and Tomlinsons 'Total Hire & Sales', now at Victory Road, is the longest establsihed plant hire company in Derby serving the needs of the construction industry over a wide area.

The parent company developed further over the following years and has made a large mark in the field of industrial building, erecting several warehouses and factories in Derbyshire.

GF Tomlinson died in 1947. He could trace his roots in Derby back three generations to William Tomlinson, a highway surveyor born in 1762 in Duffield and who oversaw the alterations and improvements to the Derby to Duffield turnpike. Astonishingly, three generations of the founder's family would follow *him* in the business: his sons George and Cyril who died in 1968 and 1976 respectively; George's son Peter who was Chairman until his retirement in 1996 and most recently Cyril's son Martin Tomlinson who joined the firm in 1967. Martin is now Company Secretary working with Chairman Barry Sewards and Construction Director Roy Collis to head a dedicated professional team capable of undertaking building contracts as diverse as new offices for British Midland Airways at Donington or the restoration of grade one listed building obtaining contracts ranging from thousands to millions of pounds in value.

Still based in City Road, Derby today the Tomlinson Group plc also has offices and depots in Birmingham, Suffolk and Hereford taking on contracts covering a third of England. The large modern business provides an astonishing testament to the entrepreneurial spirit of its founder George Frank Tomlinson.

*Top right: Peter Tomlinson. **Above left:** British Midland Airways office at Donington Hall. **Left:** The theatre in the Derby Dance Centre, converted from an old church. **Below:** Martin Tomlinson, Company Secretary.*

'Go suck a Zube!' was once a common remark that has since been replaced in modern language. Pity, it was preferable to the expression used today to tell someone to go away. That also contains a four letter word as the main thrust of its message, but it is not one to be dwelled upon here. The Zube was the throat sweet made by FW Hampshire in the silk mill the company took over from English Sewing Cotton in 1908. A major fire, a hazard all too common in factories that began life in the Industrial Revolution, nearly finished the business before it had become properly established. The fire had started in the adjacent Sowter's Flour Mill. The old silk mill was in danger of being lost when one of the main walls collapsed. The prompt action of Derby Borough Fire Brigade saved the day. There was enough left for a rebuilding programme, though the original five storeys were reduced to three. FW Hampshire concocted medicines at those premises until the 1920s. Production then moved to Sinfin Lane, to the south of Derby, where this late 1930s picture was taken. Hygiene was an important feature in such an industry. Any suggestion of contamination would have been a body blow to the business. Workers who came anywhere near to the vats and tubs used in the preparation of Hampshire's medicines had to wear caps and chemists' style white coats. The company was taken over by Reckitt and Colman in the 1970s.

Well steeled against adversity

I t's an ill wind they say, but it was blowing pretty chilly in the winter of 1973-74. Forming any new business is a risky adventure, but never more so than at that time. The whole decade was one that was full of industrial unrest. Strikes abounded and companies felt the pinch of recession. Power shortages meant electricity cuts and for a while, the country went on a three day week. Heath, Wilson and Callaghan all bought their prime ministerial might to bear, but it was not until Margaret Thatcher swept to power in 1979 that the weight of the unions was brought to heel. By then for many the damage was done. The mighty Rolls Royce company crashed in 1971 and eventually the Ilkeston factory closed. Arthur Spencer, a local man born in Belper, had managed the Ilkeston factory tool room, although offered another post at a different site within the company group. Arthur decided to back his own abilities and formed Park Engineering (Derby) Ltd on Nottingham Road. He took the name from the old Park Foundry where his father had worked.

But one of the many winters of discontent in the 1970s was the time Arthur chose to set up his company. Some may have questioned his timing but no one could fault his effort. He was fortunate to have the backing of a strong and supportive family. Without the sterling support of his wife Olga and son Rory and the business acumen of cousin John Holmes, who knows how it could have turned out? However they pulled together, as only a good family can. Just after Christmas 1973 Rory was handed a broom and given the job of sweeping the workshop floor and of disposing of all the accumulated rubbish. Olga set to work with scrubbing brush and disinfectant, scrubbing down the walls with copious amounts of water and elbow grease.

Olga says that the smell of Dettol even today reminds her of that time and how the Christmas turkey leftovers came in very useful for their pack ups for lunch, whilst they prepared the premises so that Park Engineering was ready to open early in the new year of 1974.

John Holmes was a director of the new company, he brought his commercial and legal experience to underpin the vast experience that Arthur Spencer had gained in his time at Rolls Royce. Olga Spencer became company secretary and is now its Chairperson. In the early days the company mainly dealt in mild steel, manufacturing sheet and plate metalwork. Stick welding was performed by means of a manual metal arc process. Modern techniques mean that the company has now

Left: Incinerator hood.
Below: Asquith Radial Drill refurbished after the workshop fire.

introduced welding by MIG, metal inert gas and TIG, tungsten inert gas. It also uses industrial glues and resins.
Materials are more varied, there is still plenty of mild steel in use but Park Engineering has developed the additional use of Stainless Steel, Aluminium, Nimonic as well as other materials. But the current days nearly never materialised.

Within 18 months of production beginning the company was hit by a fire and suffered the restrictions of the three day week and its power cuts. Fortunately managing director Arthur Spencer had good friends to turn to. Other companies rallied round. During the electricity shortages similar companies used whichever workshop had power to do their drilling or welding. This community spirit was unusual in business but it was necessary to keep everyone afloat. When the fire occurred on 17th August 1975 it gutted the workshop. Again friends and employees responded magnificently. Park

Engineering was up and running at full capacity within a month. After such traumatic beginnings it was only right that fortune should smile on the company. What began as a small venture began to blossom. Initially there was a single tradesman employed in the workshop during the first month which was increased to three with one additional clerical employee. By the end of the first year it would have been difficult to prophesy the business

Top: Work begins on clearing up after the devastating fire on 17th August 1975. **Above left:** *The exterior of the building following the fire.* **Below:** *The premises begin to take shape less than a month after the fire.*

in the 21st century. Park Engineering now employs 14 people and deals with such large clients as the Local Authority, Toyota, Rolls Royce, the Aerospace industry and other blue chip companies. The present managing director Rory Spencer spent his early student days doing the weeding, carrying out painting on finished jobs as well as getting the fish and chips for everyone. This would be good training for the future managing director although he did not think so at the time. The management philosophy instilled in those early days remains today, to supply the customer with an excellent service that delivers the right job at the right time and at the right price. Although speed and efficiency does not mean a reduction in quality, the company was BSI registered in 1990 and major clients supply Park Engineering with much repeat business, that in itself is a testament to the standards it achieves. Such blue chip corporations would not have any compunction in going elsewhere for their ducting, steelwork, platforms and maintenance if the service did not come up to scratch.

Rory succeeded his father as managing director when in his father suddenly died in 1990. Paul Wagg, who joined the company from leaving school, became the production director. As a

family firm that built its resilience to adversity in those troubled days of the 70s, Park Engineering offers a professional and friendly face. The quick and efficient way it conducts its business is a fine legacy to leave to the next generation of Spencers. Rory has no wish to force his two sons or daughter into the company, but he would not be disappointed to find the name of Spencer MD on the office door well into this century. Whether the name was prefixed by Mr or Ms would make no difference. All he hopes for is that whoever takes on the job acknowledges the debt owed to Arthur and Olga Spencer and their Uncle John. By the way whoever takes the exalted chair needs to get the chips in first.

Above: *The John Bakewell Gates refurbished for Derby Borough Council in 1978.*
Left: *From left to right, Mr Edward Poxon, Director, Mr AGB Wood, International Ceramics and Managing Director Mr Arthur Spencer inspect a finished order.*
Below: *One of the many fire escapes designed, manufactured and installed by the firm.*

Supporting the law for over 150 years

The legal profession is one of the most varied you could hope to join. It is a world where documents have a life, because each one represents someone's hopes, fears or aspirations. They can bring sorrow or joy. In each solicitor's day there is a sense of purpose, a feeling of having been of real service to a fellow human being. The ordinary citizen lacks the experience of the trained legal mind when faced with some of the major decisions in life. It is then that the solicitor's office comes into its own. A will may seem simple enough, but it needs someone to know what he is doing to help draw it up. The problems of inheritance tax and trusts are everyday problems to the solicitor, but without that expert help families could find themselves in a real pickle. House conveyancing is such a traumatic and potentially tricky area that it is one definitely best left to the professional. Who would want to risk the frightening prospect of facing a court room without legal support? Only the arrogant or foolhardy. If corporate giants turn their business contracts over to the legal eagles then the ordinary citizen should do the same with anything that might have implications for the future. You would not dream of pulling your own teeth or teaching yourself to a science degree, so why the reticence in drawing on other people's skills in the legal world? Certain solicitors have specialist skills and their legal partners can draw on these to offer the very best service they can.

Such is the case at Moody and Woolley. Not only does the firm have the expertise, it has the experience. To be particular, it has over a century and a half of it. Queen Victoria was in her mid 20s when Frederick Baker set up as a solicitor in Bank Chambers, Cornmarket in 1846. When John Moody joined Mr Baker at 20 Cornmarket in 1861 the firm became Baker and Moody. The older man died of rheumatic fever in 1864 and John Moody carried on singlehandedly. The business expanded and Moody gained a new partner in William Woolley in 1884. The names of Moody and Woolley were joined in the firm's title and has continued to be used to this day.

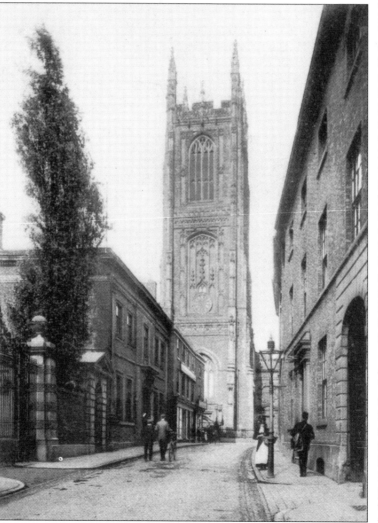

Mr Moody died in 1889 and William Woolley continued on his own. At the turn of the century other partners were taken into the business and the firm grew in size and influence. Larger premises were needed to handle the level of business coming their way. A move was made to 40 St Mary's Gate in 1912, the week the Titanic sank! It was a grand Georgian residence, built in 1800, where the firm remains to this day.

Although both William Woolley's sons joined the firm, only Leslie stayed long enough to have any significant influence. He became a partner in 1929 when most of the work in the office was still being recorded in longhand.

Top: John Moody, who joined the firm in 1861.
Above centre: *St Mary's Gate c.1912, the year the firm took over the building on the right.*

new technology have made an enormous difference to the efficiency of the firm. It has kept abreast of developments, including such massively influential legislation as the 2000 Human Rights Act. The countless generations of Derby families who return again and again to the firm is testament to its long dedication to making their private and business lives run as smoothly and trouble-free as possible.

Top: *Members of the firm's staff in the late 1960s.*
Above left: *Moody & Woolley's present day offices in St Mary's Gate.* ***Below:*** *Today's partners, Ian Griffiths and Julie Marson with the coveted Investors in People Award in January 2000.*

Typewriters, the high tech machines of the time, were only starting to make a limited appearance in those days and until 1930 the firm had just one telephone in a specially soundproofed booth.

Leslie Woolley served his country as a captain in the Royal Artillery and after the war returned to the firm and served it well until his death in 1968.

Moody and Woolley celebrated 150 years of legal service in Derby in 1996. It was an celebration attended by more than 100 members of firm (past and present), the oldest of whom could still remember the days when a man was employed specifically to keep the coal piled on the open fires situated in every room. Today, Derby's second oldest law firm is as strong as ever, and whilst retaining its air of history and continuity, changes in the law and

The Fire Brigade in Derby

The Derby Fire Brigade came into existence in 1837 as a direct result of Government policy to impose a requirement on Local Authorities of the day to take responsibility for fires in their area. This was due in the main to a large number of fires throughout the country, and the inadequate arrangements with insurance and local run brigades. These local run brigades were being administered mainly by the churches of the day. The response to calls came from church bell ringing and shouting for help. Volunteers were paid 6d and a drink to 'man the pumps'. Derby had five separate fire engines up to 1837 operated by the churches of All Saints, St Werburghs, St Johns, St Peters and St Marys.

When officials of the local council decided they ought to follow the guide issued by the Government, they ordered an inspection of the fire engines. They were advised that only two were serviceable to operate in the new organisation (these engines were in fact horse drawn and hand operated pumps.) Both engines were housed and operated from premises in Tenant Street in Derby. A person was employed as the 'engine man' and lived close by the engine house building. It is interesting to note that his wages were paid out of the salary of the Mayor. An early problem to the brigade was the provision of water for firefighting and although the area of the Market Place had the nearby river Derwent, all other outlying areas had to rely on 'bucketing' from any available supply.

The 'engine house' was relocated around 1861 into Full Street with a purpose built house in which the engineer lived on site. A lack of investment in new equipment resulted in a slow deterioration of the engines up to the disastrous fire suffered by the Town Hall in 1866. From this came a new commitment and new fire engines were purchased, firemen employed and water mains laid. This period up to 1891 saw many changes in Derby including the growth of the railways and other industries. Many fires still occurred and part of the learning was to lobby authorities to abolish the style of building properties too close together, using poor construction and not including fire breaks particularly in thatch roofs. The introduction of 'steam' fire pumps provided spectacular viewing as engines careered through the town behind galloping horses.

In 1891 Derby provided a magnificent new fire station on Jury Street in the central area of the town. This purpose built accommodation housed three fire engines with firemen's houses attached to the rear stretching towards Walker Lane and Willow Row. There were many outbuildings to cater for horses, hay and animals, as it was also the practice for the fire brigade to dispose of unwanted animals at this time. This unusual service remained well into the next century and the poor unfortunate animals were disposed of by electrocution. During this period the Police and Fire Brigade shared duties and firemen were expected to transport prisoners to attend Nottingham Court. The houses on Jury Street all had bells to summon crews and you can imagine the effect on the rest of these families during busy times.

During the first world war the brigade was badly depleted as a result of military service but luckily there were no major fires at that time. This period also saw the introduction of motorised appliances with pneumatic tyres. Some old crews still preferred the horses and it took many years to overcome this hatred of modern technology. Inevitably the horse drawn engines were withdrawn and new appliances purchased. Derby was now the proud owner of two pumping appliances and one high rise ladder.

Below: *Central fire station in Jury Street, built in 1891.*

Derby saw action during the second world war but perhaps not on the scale of some other areas. Larger cities like Coventry suffered constant attacks and as a result fire appliances from all over the Midlands, including Derby went to help fight the fires. This time also saw a massive influx of personnel including full time, part time and members of the Auxiliary Fire Service using the 'green goddess' major pumps (these appliances and crews remained attached to Jury Street on a part time basis up until the mid sixties.) It was after the war that Derby began to take on the size of a moderate town and the resources of the brigade were increased to reflect this. The Fire Services Act of 1947 created the County Borough of Derby Fire Brigade, which replaced the National Fire Service that had so gallantly carried us through the war years.

Derby continued to grow and it became obvious that the Jury Street station was not best suited to reach other areas of the town due to the increase in traffic congestion. The suburbs began to grow in both residential and industrial risks and another station was obviously required. The new fire station at Nottingham Road was opened in 1951 providing two more fire appliances. Derby was now in line with other comparable towns in fact in 1963 they went one better and opened another fire station at Ascot Drive which became the brigade headquarters. The middle of the 1960s saw the large scale flooding around the area of Chester Green to which the brigade responded for days on end in the rescue of residents and animals.

The old station at Jury Street began to show its age in accommodating modern appliances and was finally replaced in 1968 by a new station at Kingsway. This completed the strategy of three stations all on main traffic routes providing a rapid response to the suburbs or town centre.

The Borough Brigade existed until 1974 when local government re-organisation required it to join forces with the Derbyshire Fire Service that had covered the rest of the county at that time. The new Derbyshire Fire Service name remained until recent years when the addition of 'Rescue' was adopted by most fire brigades. The new headquarters opened at Littleover in Derby where it remains to this day.

Derby still has the three fire stations although additional facilities at Kingsway now include a purpose built training complex for recruits and also breathing apparatus hot fire training. The headquarters provides accommodation for residential courses of all kinds. All emergency calls are received at headquarters and appliances mobilised to incidents covering the whole county of Derbyshire. Close liaison is maintained at all times with police and ambulance services to provide a joint approach to emergencies and inter agency co-operation.

The provision of service today is a far cry from the firemen of yesteryear and equipment and resources reflect the demand to control and deal with a wide variety of calls for help from the community. A much greater education of the public towards fire safety now takes place and every fire station, plus community teams target all generations in a way that can be understood.

Performance indicators now measure a modern service and Derbyshire is up amongst the top brigades for achieving the marks set by the Home Office. The number of fatalities as a result of fire are down in the brigade which is against the national trend. The cost of running the brigade per head of population is below that of most others in the country. Recruitment now embraces all communities and as a result the percentage of both women and ethnic groups working with the service is above that of other brigades. Derby has played a significant part in the progress since the hand pumps of 1837 and the service is committed to serve and care for the population of this fine city.

Above: *Modern-day firefighters ready for action.*
Top: *The latest high-rise special appliance.*

Caring for those who once cared for us

Advances in medicine have done us all a favour. We stay fitter and live longer than our parents or their parents before them. But even governments regard Britain's ageing population as a problem that the 21st century must tackle. A problem? The nation's senior citizens should be up in arms over such a description. Yet it is a sad fact of life for many that they become thought of as a burden on the state and a nuisance to the family. They have brought up families, nurtured them, paid their dues to society and are then left to feel unwanted. Thankfully, such cases are a minority, but who cares for the carer when no one else can? In Victorian times the elderly were shunted off to the workhouse if they had no relatives to help or insufficient funds to pay for private care. The second world war became another factor in determining their welfare. Many were made homeless by bombing raids and others lost sons and daughters who might have been able to help. Walter Hall, a Methodist minister, recognised the need to establish help for such people. In

1943 he founded Methodist Homes and opened the first one at Ryelands in Wallington.

Thanks to Reverend Hall we now have a movement that cares for over 5,000 people. Spurred by their Christian concern for others, the workers in the organisation strive to improve the quality of life of older folk. The support is given in residential homes, offering 24 hour comfort. Residents of these homes were among the country's first to be encouraged to personalise their own rooms, rather than rely on institutional furniture. Community based support is also given to those living in their own homes or in sheltered accommodation. Specialist help is given to those who are suffering dementia.

The Methodist Homes' head office moved to Derby from Westminster in 1991. It fulfils the vision of Walter Hall in providing person centred care for the elderly with the true Christian ethic of love thy neighbour.

Above: *The Rev Walter Hall in 1958.* ***Left:*** *A resident and one of the many volunteers brighten up a home with pot plants.* ***Below:*** *Residents on one of the Sheltered Housing Schemes.*

Terotechnology for the new millennium

The company known today as Greenbank Terotech began in 1954 in premises in Blackburn when Jack Whittaker and Harry joined forces in business. At first, design was the main product of Greenbank Engineering, but in 1957 the company decided to manufacture in their own right and soon industrial driers were being produced and subsequently also ancillary equipment used in drying lines. Very soon the company was exporting its products.

Expansion followed rapidly and new premises were acquired in Blackburn and Burnley. In 1965 the Cast Basalt business was acquired and run from these sites. Drying machinery production was concentrated in Blackpool.

In 1971 the company went public under the name Greenbank Industrial Holdings and since that time has had over 500 people on its payroll. The 'Heavy Industries' division of the company evolved and Greenbank 'Cast Basalt' Engineering Company was born, which had subsidiary companies in the US, South Africa, Australia and India. The 'Heavy Industrial Division' was formed in 1981 having its two main bases at Blackburn, these were Greenbank Terotech Limited and Greenbank Darwen Ltd. Following a merger in 1988, the engineering assets were bought by the management team in 1990 and engineering facilities were concentrated on the Burnley site. In 1995 the operation was transferred to Derby when the enterprise was taken over by Prospect Industries Limited before becoming part of the Shaw Group.

A holding company, Greenbank Acquisitions Corporation made up of Greenbank Management and its sister company in America, bought outright the company in 1998.

The company offers well-equipped facilities, including a 300 tonne press as well as purpose built machinery for the manufacture of specialised pipework and the installation of lining systems. The company acquired PAC Engineering Linings and its former Director, Peter Cobham is now Group Sales Director of Greenbank Terotech Ltd.

In September 1999 Greenbank established a Systems division which specialises in electronic control systems, and which supports the company with turnkey ash handling projects, as well as providing back-up for Greenbank's new ash and moisture analysis equipment.

In November 1999 Greenbank acquired the assets of Benchmark Solutions Ltd, which design, build and install turnkey conveyor systems as well as providing a refurbishing and maintenance service to the bulk handling industry.

Above: Design systems. **Below left:** *Manual welding operation.* **Below:** *Automated welding operation.*

A happy, mainly female, band of workers awaiting the royal visit of the Duke of York to Ley's foundries in 1933.

Acknowledgments

The publishers would like to thank

WW Winter Limited
Tony Bowler

Thanks are also due to
Andrew Mitchell who penned the editorial text and
Judith Dennis for her copywriting skills